In Search of Me

A JOURNEY OF FAITH AND DISCOVERY

J.L. Stoenner

WestBow Press books may be ordered through booksellers or by contacting:

WestBow Press
A Division of Thomas Nelson & Zondervan
1663 Liberty Drive
Bloomington, IN 47403
www.westbowpress.com
1 (866) 928-1240

ISBN: 978-1-5127-1934-5 (sc)
ISBN: 978-1-5127-1935-2 (hc)
ISBN: 978-1-5127-1933-8 (e)

Library of Congress Control Number: 2015918671

Print information available on the last page.

WestBow Press rev. date: 11/16/2015

Dedication

I would like to dedicate this book first and foremost to Jesus Christ. To Him be all the glory.

Secondly, to my family and friends who have helped me along the way.

Acknowledgements

First and foremost, I would like to thank my wonderful husband for all his support and encouragement during the writing of this book; especially in reference to pulling extra childcare duty and doing extra housework so I could write. Also, for being one of my editors! You are a strong man of faith, and so talented, generous, and supportive. Your love and support has meant so much to me. Thank you for helping to make one of my dreams of becoming a published author come true.

Next, I would like to thank Dori Abbott for also helping me with editing, especially with the introduction and first couple of chapters, which really helped with the smooth flow of the rest of the book. I know we both recognize God's providence in bringing us together when He did, and I am so thankful—not just because you are great at what you do and I really enjoy your company, but because you have inspired me into a deeper level of faith. To see how you trust God through all your trials has inspired me greatly.

I would also like to thank Hannah Jones for helping me come up with some cover ideas, and Jessica Appleby for shooting my cover photo! I cherish your friendships. Thank you Keith Durham for donating a lovely author photo of me. Also, thanks to all those who helped with the cost of getting the publishing process started.

A big thanks to Rob Rucci, for writing an excellent forward. I really appreciate it a lot. I never cease to be amazed at how, during the writing of my book, the sermons you preached quite often lined up with what I was writing about at the time. It makes me think about how powerful and far reaching our faith is, more than we will ever know in this life.

Lastly, I would like to thank Westbow Press for being so great to work with. Everyone has been very helpful, professional and friendly.

Foreword

You've probably heard the adage, "Experience is the best teacher." In fact, you may be living proof of it. I certainly am. At times, experience is a great mentor, like an old friend guiding us through a difficult passage in life. Yet it can also be a sudden and not so subtle alarm, warning us of peril ahead.

However it comes, easy or hard, gradual or swift, experience is instruction meant to educate and mature us for the journey ahead and therefore, we are wise to heed its lessons.

Some of the greatest lessons learned, in my own life, have been through the experiences of others, as I've journeyed down the path of life with them. In fact, there is much to be learned simply by being attentive and observant of those with which we have the privilege of experiencing life alongside.

In her first book, Jen Stoenner opens up the pages of her heart and unselfishly allows the reader a front row seat in the classroom of her most poignant life experiences. As a missionary, wife, and mother with an undying wanderlust for God's will to be expressed in and through her life, no matter where that leads her, Jen takes us on an adventure with a vulnerability and honesty that is both refreshing and captivating.

Knowing Jen and her family personally, I have watched her leverage every drop of her considerable talent and energy and passion to their greatest effect in the lives of those around her. The beauty of this writing is that it is an invitation for you to do the same, to learn and grow from her personal challenges, failures, fears, and triumphs.

Even though you may never have met her, you will become a trusted friend as you journey with Jen through the pages of her life, untethered by the pretense or formality that often comes when meeting someone new. So turn the page and enjoy the journey. I certainly have.

Rob Rucci, Founder and Pastor
Upcountry Church, Travelers Rest, S.C.
2015

Introduction

This is the story of how I came to realize, without a shadow of a doubt, that **God is love** and that **He loves *me***. Such simple statements, but what a profound difference they have made in my life! And what a profound difference they can make in your life as well. When we truly understand who God is, that His very essence is love, and when we open ourselves up and truly accept and receive His unconditional love for us—well, that changes everything.

Many of us grew up in church singing, "Jesus loves me this I know, for the Bible tells me so..." But I wonder how many of us really believe this. I mean *really.* What does God's love for me look like? What does it feel like? How do I know I have really taken God at His word, believing that He indeed loves me? These are some of the questions that we will explore together in this book.

I share my story here in hopes that many will come to a deep and personal relationship with Jesus Christ and catch a glimpse of the height, the depth, and the length of His immeasurable love for us. I also hope that my story will help many learn how to daily receive and live in God's great love.

In this book I will recount moments where my heart was being awakened to the wonderful, loving nature of God, and to my true identity and purpose in Him. I will also recount moments where God and the conscious awareness of His great love for me brought me deep healing, restoration and freedom. Included also are some reflective questions for you, the reader, as well as some correlating Scriptures to ponder on.

The title of this book, *In Search of Me,* has two different meanings. One meaning is my personal journey to discover who I am and my true purpose; the other is God's successful attempts to find me and reveal Himself and His purposes to me. The most beautiful part is that I indeed found myself and my purpose in Him and I know He wants you to do the same.

I hope as you read this book God touches your heart in a powerful way. May your feet be firmly rooted and grounded in His love for you, and may your eyes be opened more and more to the beautiful, loving nature of God, your true identity, and to His good and pleasing and perfect will for your life. Much love, Jennie.

Chapter 1

"Life has to be better than this. There has to be more to life than this."

It was my senior year of high school, and it wasn't starting off very well. I was very aware of the fact that I had some major life decisions to make, and I didn't feel up to the task. At this point in my life, I saw the future as one big competition. It was my belief that the people who were happy in life were the people who were successful in their career of choice. I wanted to be a movie actress. I wasn't confident in my ability to be successful as an actress, though. I didn't believe I was good enough.

Actually, at the time, I didn't feel like I would ever really be good enough. As a result, my dream of a happy life as an actress was like a big, mean bully, taunting me with something I would never have. As askew as my life view was at the time, it was how I felt. It was my reality. So you can see my dilemma. I was struggling because I felt like my dreams would only remain just that: dreams. This didn't give me much excitement about the future. Then began my desperate cry for help.

I'd grown up in church thinking that I was a Christian. Now that I look back, though, I'm not so sure. My life didn't exactly reflect someone who had genuine faith. I may have had a bit more of a guilty conscience than some of my peers, but I think that's about it. I will say that being raised in church benefited me in that when the whole weight of my dilemma became too much to bear, my first instinct was to cry out to God for help. "Life has to be better than this! There has to be more to life than this!" Better than what? More than what? A big competition where only those who are good enough and talented enough get to be truly happy?

I felt as if I was at a fork in the road and I had to decide whether I would fight for the life I wanted or give up on my dreams, settling for second best and condemning myself to a life of slowly dying inside. Well, I wasn't willing to give up. Somewhere deep inside of me was a small glimmer of hope. After I cried out to God (and just plain cried), I felt better. At the time I didn't receive any answers—or so I thought. But in that moment, I didn't mind. I had a deep feeling of peace. It was as if God was saying to me, "Don't worry. I've got this. You're gonna be okay."

Little did I know all the things that were soon to unfold as a result of that one little prayer (as if prayer is ever little). I would soon find out that I didn't have within myself what it takes to have the exciting, adventurous, happy life that I so desired. My world was about to change. On that fateful day, after I got home from school, while lying on my bed with the covers over my head, my life took a turn for the best.

I don't know what I expected to happen after that, or if I even expected anything at all, but God was on the move. It was October, 2000, about a month after I prayed that prayer, when my mom informed me that the Celebrant Singers were coming to our church that week. She asked me if I wanted to go with her to see them. The Celebrant Singers are a nondenominational music and mission team based out of California who travel all over the world, sharing the gospel and strengthening the church through music, preaching, and prayer.

They had come to my church when I was younger, but I didn't remember much about them. I didn't have anything else better to do, so I went along. By the end of the night, my poor mother's shoulder was covered in my snot and tears. These people had something special, something beautiful, something *more*. They were filled with joy, passionate about life, and in love with Jesus! I had met people before who seemed joyful and passionate about life, but not many who attributed it to Jesus like these missionaries did.

When the director of the team spoke, he talked about the importance of having a personal relationship with Jesus Christ—how we need to put our faith in Christ, commit our lives to Him, strive to live for Him, and love Him first. He explained how Jesus came into the world to die for our sins and how through repentance of our sins and faith in Him and His life, death, and resurrection, we would receive forgiveness of our sins and eternal life in heaven. Our stories would change from being lost and being slaves to sin who are without God and without hope in the world to being found, forgiven, and redeemed, able to live the lives we were meant to live for God.

At the end of the concert, there was a time of prayer. They invited people in the crowd to commit their lives to Jesus for the first time or to rededicate their lives to Him; they also asked whether anyone had any special prayer requests. We were told to raise a hand if this was our desire, and then a team member would come and pray with us individually. I was confused. Like I said, I had always believed in Jesus, and I considered myself a Christian. So I didn't think I fit into the first two categories. I raised my hand for prayer, and a woman from the team came around to pray for me.

She asked what I wanted prayer for. I said, "I don't know." So she just began to pray whatever God put on her heart to pray. I can't remember the exact words, but I know it was comforting—like a small tangible touch from God. I wasn't accustomed to people praying out loud for me, but I loved it! I loved the whole night! I felt peace and love and joy like I'd never felt before. I didn't want it to end!

After they finished praying for people in the crowd, a woman from the team got up and made an announcement. She asked whether there was anyone eighteen or older who could sing, play an instrument, or run sound and lighting equipment who might be interested in traveling with them over the summer. I felt my ears perk up. The announcer went on to say that they would be holding auditions that night immediately following her announcement for anyone who was interested.

I had just turned eighteen about a month prior, and I had several years of experience singing in school choirs, various drama productions, and church. I couldn't think of anything else I would rather do with my summer, so I went up to audition. I was never very good at "on the spot" auditions, but I gave it my best shot. On top of being nervous, I was really congested from all the crying I had been doing earlier that night. Needless to say, it wasn't my best performance. They told me not to worry and said that I could take an application and send it in later along with a vocal recording.

During the next month, my church choir helped me prepare a few songs to send in. I was *really* excited. Finally, after a long wait, the call came. They said they didn't feel my voice was ready, but they did have a lighting-technician position available if I would be interested. I had never run lights before, and I wasn't the most technically savvy kid out there, but I didn't care. I very willingly accepted the position. Looking back now, I know I had no idea what I was getting myself into or about the dramatic life change that was about to take place. I knew that these people had something I wanted, though, and that was enough for me.

I left for my first mission trip the day after I graduated from high school. It was intense, challenging, and amazing—more than I could have hoped for. It was actually during the ten-day training camp in California, before we left for mission, when I realized that maybe I should genuinely commit my life to Jesus, because *really*, even though I believed in Him, I had never truly surrendered my life to Him, and I was starting to learn that this is what it meant to be a true follower of Jesus (2 Corinthians 5:15). It was during an evening devotional when the speaker said, "If you're not sure where you stand spiritually, you might want to take care of that now before we go out on the road, because there is a major spiritual battle going on, and you want to make sure you're covered." Nobody prayed with me to completely surrender my life to Jesus. I just prayed quietly myself. My prayer went a little something like this: "Lord, I recognize I am a sinner in need of saving, and I am very sorry for my sins. Jesus, I believe You are the Christ, the Savior of the world; that You died for the sins of the world; and that whoever believes in You shall not die but have eternal life. Jesus, I believe in You, and I am asking You now to come into my heart and be my Lord and Savior. I commit my life to You. I want to live for You. You are worthy of all my life and love. Amen." This was the beginning of my walk with Jesus. Ultimately, I also ended up as a vocalist with the group, which was like icing on the cake!

Here are just a few of my journal entries from that summer:

(June 6, 2001)

I can honestly say now, God has already touched my heart and changed me (2 Corinthians 5:17). I know that I still have a long way to go, but I am willing to travel the distance. I pray that God helps me never to forget what I've learned this summer and what I've experienced. And if I'm ever lost, I pray that I will read this journal entry and rediscover how much God loves me, and remember that He has a plan for my life. Let me surrender to Him, trust in Him, and know that He will never leave me. He loves me with an awesome love.

(June 8, 2001)

I cried today during devotionals because I felt God's presence so strongly, and because I am so happy that I'm here. This is the most amazing thing I've ever experienced. We've only been here for four days, but God has touched my heart in such a way that I can honestly say I'm a different person. I have a whole new attitude about life.

(August 29, 2001)

I feel that I've learned and grown so much. I have confidence that I will never forget what I've learned this summer or the work that God has done in my heart. I know I still have a long way to go, and it's my constant prayer that I continue to grow. Instead of being fearful of the future, I am excited! I am excited for what God has planned for my life. God has given me so much faith, hope, and love. I'm on fire with a burning desire to draw closer to the heart of my Savior.

I returned home, a completely different person than when I left. My life didn't revolve around *me* anymore. I had fallen madly in love with Jesus, the lover of my soul, and I was determined to follow Him for the rest of my life. After I committed my life to Christ, I soon learned that the purpose of life isn't just to be happy. God wants us to know Him and to make Him known. Through many personal experiences, I've also learned that when we are truly living for God, deep joy and fulfillment are the natural result.

Throughout the rest of this book, I will be sharing some of my journal entries from the first six years of my journey with Jesus after I returned home from my first mission trip. To assist you on your own journey with Jesus, questions and Scriptures will be presented at the end of each chapter for reflection. Prepare your heart, and let the journey begin…

Chapter 2

(October 23, 2001)

Today I woke up in a fairly good mood. The first thing I did was grab one of the recommended books that I'm reading in my preparation to become a licensed massage therapist. Then I grabbed the article I've been reading about prayer and discernment.

I took both of them upstairs and positioned myself into a cozy reading position on the couch in our living room. I read the textbook relating to massage first. It was very interesting, and got me even more excited about massage school. Then I read the rest of the article on prayer and discernment. Reading this article helped me to confirm the path that I feel I'm supposed to take! I've decided that I don't want to pursue acting as a career anytime in the immediate future. I realize that it's not something that is super high on my priority list anymore. Don't get me wrong—I enjoy acting, but not enough to make a career out of it right now. There are other things that I want to focus on first. First and foremost, I want to get closer to Jesus. I feel like acting would get in the way of that, at least for right now. I would also like to find a nice place to work as a massage therapist, get a family started, and get involved with some sort of ministry. Then maybe I will think about acting again, if I still feel as passionate about it and it's something God leads me to do.

(January 11, 2002)

I haven't written for a long time. Too long. I'm feeling very lonely right now. I'm at home and I'm struggling. I'm having a difficult time transitioning back into the life I knew with my newfound faith. I don't know if I expected it to be easy to live out being a committed Christian, or if it's just a lot harder than I realized it would be. Regardless, I had a negative experience at home and I decided to take a drive.

I ended up going to McDonald's to get an ice cream. On the way there I got stuck by a train, so I put my car in park and just started crying. When I finally pulled up to the window at McDonald's, I guess the guy could tell that I had been crying because he said, "Oh come on, smile. It can't be that bad." I gave him a weak smile, took my ice-cream cone, and drove off. I immediately burst into tears and cried even harder than before. This time, not because I was sad. It was actually the opposite. What that guy said was exactly what I needed to hear. I knew it was a message from God for me. I knew it was God telling me that He was with me like He promised He would be, and that I would be okay.

I know that right now is a very important time in my life; a turning point if you will. I'm very excited for what God has in store for my life in Him. I've been confessing to God in prayer that I want to live BIG for Him, and I feel that this is exactly what He is calling me to do. My deepest desire is to answer that call with all my heart; with my entire being.

In other news, God has been faithful to help me find a church here where I can move forward and grow in my faith. He's also given me some friends that I can grow with. I am very thankful!

At this time in my life I did anything that I could to fuel my newly discovered faith. I often found myself reading my Bible, reading Christian books about faith, listening to praise and worship music, going to church meetings, and talking to other Christians about faith and what God was teaching me. I was continually finding myself in situations where a door would open up for me to share the gospel with people and explain various Biblical principles to help them with their problems. I believed with all my heart (and I still do) that Jesus is the answer to all of our problems and questions about life.

Questions:

1. What do you believe about Jesus?

2. Have you ever committed your life to Jesus? If no, why not?

3. What are your top five priorities in life?

4. What is your number one desire in life?

5. What support do you have to help you grow in your faith (church, friends, etc.)? If you don't have any support, what will you do this week to change that?

Chapter 3

I recently started occasionally attending an Assembly of God church in my hometown, and even started helping with the youth group there. In March, the church had a guest speaker who came and spoke on who the Holy Spirit is and what it means to be baptized in the Spirit.

When he finished sharing, he invited anyone who was interested in being baptized in the Holy Spirit to come to the front of the church. I decided to respond. When I arrived at the front, I laid down on the stairs around the stage and buried my head in my arms. The speaker then invited people to come and pray with those of us who were gathered at the front.

Before long a lady came and prayed with me. It was the first time I had ever heard anyone pray "in the Spirit" (some refer to this as speaking in tongues). She would pray in the Spirit, and then talk to me and tell me that God wants to use me. She also said that I shouldn't be afraid because He will never leave me. Then she would cry and thank God for me. When she spoke, I knew it wasn't her words but the Spirit of God inspiring her. I couldn't contain myself, and started weeping. Whenever she spoke, it was as if God was speaking directly to me, answering questions I had deep in my heart.

I had been praying a lot about how I wanted to live big for God. God spoke through this woman, saying that He had wonderful plans for me and that He wanted me to trust Him. He was telling me that He knew my heart was willing and that He would help me. After hearing these words, it was as if I was surrounded by a bright light and I couldn't feel the ground beneath me. The only words that I can think of to describe what I felt in this moment are "perfect peace." It was incredible! I felt so unworthy to be hearing God speak so clearly to me, and I just kept crying. A few more people came and prayed for me. Eventually, I stopped crying and just laid there in perfect peace, feeling God's presence all around me. I didn't have a care in the world—I simply allowed God to hold me. It was *so* wonderful, and I didn't want it to end.

Not long after this experience, I experienced times of feeling very close to Jesus and also times of great frustration. The frustration came because I was struggling with being consistent in studying the scriptures and spending time with Jesus. I knew that when I read my Bible, wrote in my journal, and prayed, I felt much better. So why was it so hard for me to do those things on a regular basis? This is a tough question and I believe the answer is different for everyone.

Basically, I was now engaged in a battle between my flesh and my spirit (Galatians 6:7-9). A life of faith is very difficult for someone who has been so accustomed to living just like everyone else "in the world," and I was that "someone" not very long ago.

I was hearing the Spirit say, "Put God first. Earnestly seek Him and never give up on your faith. Never be complacent. Never lose sight of the goal. What matters most in the life to come should be what matters most in *this* life. You mustn't be afraid. If you step out in faith, led by Me, I won't let you fall. I'll protect you and give you strength. You mustn't stray from the Word, for it is the only real truth; the only true way. Be careful what you say, because words have the power of life and death. Renew your mind by studying and meditating on the Word of God, and live out what you read."

The Holy Spirit also showed me that I wasn't letting Jesus be enough for me. I was letting too much of my sense of self-worth depend on other people. He was asking me to do whatever I needed to do to give Jesus first place in my heart and life. He told me that when I put my full trust in Him, I would *truly* know Him, and He would manifest His Spirit so strong within me that I would be used to touch a nation for Christ—even the world. He wanted me to live for Him alone, and told me that if I would only seek Him with all my heart, then all my prayers would be answered.

No more would I question or doubt; no more would I worry, seek attention, or have wandering eyes. No more would I be lazy or depressed; because His Spirit would be so alive in me, I wouldn't be able to sit still or be sad. I just needed to surrender myself completely to Him so that He could give me all of my heart's desires (and more)! He said this was going to take discipline and effort on my part, but He promised that He would help me. He also promised that it would be worth it. He told me He would change me if I let Him. However, I needed to seek the Lord with all my heart. No more exceptions, no more excuses—He wanted all of me. He wanted me to get rid of any hindrances. My heart needed purifying and my mind needed renewing. Committing my life to Christ was only the start. There was a lot of work that needed to be done in me if I was to experience this life of excitement and adventure; this life of peace, love, joy, and fulfillment—this life of "better"; this life of "more." I had some bad habits that needed breaking and it was time to get to work.

Who is the Holy Spirit?

"..The Holy Spirit is the third person of the Trinity. God the Holy Spirit can truly function as the comforter and counselor that Jesus promised He would be" (John 14:16, 26; 15:26).[1]

What is the baptism of the Holy Spirit and why do we need it?

I love how John Piper answers this question:

> The main reason we need the baptism of the Holy Spirit—the great outpouring of the Spirit, the great immersion of every part of our lives in the Spirit—is because God's aim in every part of our lives is the glory of Jesus Christ. Is your life magnifying Christ in every part? If not, pray, as I do so often, for a fresh, fuller baptism in the Holy Spirit. O Holy Spirit, come. O risen Christ, for your great name's sake, grant us a fresh baptism in your Holy Spirit...[2]

Questions:

1. What do you believe about the baptism of the Holy Spirit?

2. Have you ever received the baptism of the Holy Spirit? If yes, write a description of your experience. If not, pray and ask God to do this in your life.

3. What did you learn about God in this chapter?

Chapter 4

(May 7, 2002)

Yesterday, I went to the Assembly of God Church for a prayer meeting. Pastor John asked me if I would like prayer for anything, and of course I said, "Yes." I have so many things going on in my life right now, and I've been feeling a bit overwhelmed. After Pastor John and his wife Jody finished praying for me, I felt much better. Before I went to sit back down, Jody said something very interesting. She said, "Be on your guard, because the devil doesn't always come as an angel of darkness; sometimes he masquerades as an angel of light" (2 Corinthians 11:14). Then she said, "The devil may tempt you with a bunch of good things, but you must stay focused on the best things, or the things you know that Jesus is leading you to do."

Pastor John then said to me, "And remember, it's not what you *do* for the Lord, but *who you are*." Boy, that sure took a load off of my shoulders! I realized in that moment that I'd been under the false impression that my works gave me value in God's eyes, which simply, and thankfully, isn't true. I am a child of God, and that's what gives me value in His eyes. During prayer that same day, the Lord also revealed to me that I haven't been including Him in my life as much as I should be. I know now that I need to make more time for Him.

(May 28, 2002)

Today was a really good day. It didn't start off that way though. I was feeling discouraged because I haven't been very consistent in spending time with Jesus; I was even more frustrated because I was going over to my friend Lila's house to give her a massage, and I didn't want to go there in a down mood. Well, after I kept repeating in my mind over and over that it would be okay; that God would help me and deliver me from my discouragement just like He's delivered me in the past, I gradually began to feel better, and *better*!

By the time I arrived at Lila's house, I was actually bubbling over with joy. Lila and I always have such a nice time visiting, and sharing stories and testimonies about how God has been so faithful to us. Today I told her how God has been helping me to be careful about what I say and to see things in a more positive light. I also shared with her how the Lord is helping me trust Him more, seek greater gifts, and believe that it's possible for me to make a big difference for Him in the world.

Many people have said to me, "Be careful what you pray for." But for some reason, I often find myself praying for trials and tests. I think it's because I know that trials will help me grow in my faith, and that's the most important thing to me right now (James 1:2-4). I pray that I will never stop seeking to grow in my faith. I pray that I will never become complacent. Many times I'm apprehensive to step out of my comfort zone or to think outside the box. Yet every time I do what the Lord asks me to do (even when it's scary), He blesses me in incredible ways. I feel like I've grown tremendously these past few weeks. One thing that I'm doing more of is praising and worshipping God for His goodness, instead of whining and crying when things don't go my way. Well, I wasn't whining and crying all the time. I was just failing to bring my problems to Him and trust that He would take care of them.

Lord, I pray for Your divine intervention in these areas where I am struggling.

I pray that You will help me become strong in You instead of trusting in myself. What am I without You? I'm incomplete. You complete me. Thank You Jesus!

Questions:

1. Are you feeling overwhelmed by anything right now? If yes, write it down, then bring it to God in prayer (Phil. 4:6-7).

2. What gives you value in God's eyes?

3. Why would the devil masquerade as an angel of light? What does this mean? Hint: read 2 Corinthians 11:1-15.

4. Do you feel peace in your heart that you are including God in your life as much as you should? If your answer is "no", than what are some things you can do to include Him more?

5. Write down some ways that God has helped you grow in your faith.

6. What have you learned about God in this chapter?

Chapter 5

(June 5, 2002)

So, I just got finished catching up in a book I am reading called *10 Challenges of a World Changer* by Ron Luce. I also read several portions of Scripture and spent some time reading my journal entries from the end of April up until now. Wow! Let me tell you, after all of that I am feeling *really* inspired and excited! God is so amazing!

I am really enjoying *10 Challenges of a World Changer*. It is helping me to actually believe that I *can* make a big difference for God in the world (with God's help of course), which really excites me!

The first couple verses of Scripture that really spoke to me were John 3:3,6 which says, "Jesus replied, 'Very truly I tell you, no one can see the kingdom of God unless they are born again.... .Flesh gives birth to flesh, but the Spirit gives birth to spirit.'" So a person must be born of the Spirit to be born again, and to do this you must repent of your sins and trust in Jesus as your Lord and Savior (John 3:18). When we do this, an amazing transformation takes place—God completely changes us from the inside out. "Therefore, if anyone is in Christ, the new creation has come: The old has gone, the new is here!" (2 Corinthians 5:17)

We start over as babies in Christ, and we are to pursue spiritual growth and maturity so that we can continue to grow and mature into the people God created us to be. This turns out for our good and for His glory (Romans 6:17-18). We need to allow Jesus to mold and shape us into what He wants us to be. This surrendering of our wills isn't always easy. In fact, it will most likely be incredibly difficult. Many times it means that we will have to sacrifice some things that we really like, and even some things that we love. Jesus commands us to pick up our cross and carry it daily (Luke 9:23).

The next portion of Scripture that really spoke to me was John 1:12-13: "Yet to all who did receive him, to those who believed in his name, he gave the right to become children of God—children born not of natural descent, nor of human decision or a husband's will, but born of God." I am one of God's children! I am beginning to understand what a privilege, honor, and gift it is to be a child of God. One of the many benefits of being a child of God is that I am washed clean of my sins. As a result, I am also set free from the power of sin and death!

The next verse that really spoke to me was Matthew 22:37: "Jesus replied: 'Love the Lord your God with all your heart and with all your soul and with all your mind.' This is the first and greatest commandment." I'm learning that the relationship that God wants with me is one where I love Him with everything that I am, not holding anything back. When I do this, everything else in my life will fall into place (Matthew 6:33). I'm still learning what it looks like to live this out on a daily basis. I do know that having a relationship with God is not just following a bunch of rules and regulations, trying to be good so that God will love me more. It has nothing to do with that. God loved me before I ever gave my heart to Him and He will keep loving me no matter what. Having a personal relationship means being committed to Him and loving Him back.

I am also learning that another important part of my mission in this life as a child of God is to fulfill my role in the Body of Christ, the Church (Romans 12:5). We're all in this together. We all have a role to play in the Body of Christ. The sooner we realize this and get to it, the sooner the world will be a better place.

Finally, I read through a few journal entries from the past year where I clearly saw how the Lord has been moulding me, shaping me, and preparing me for my mission trip to El Salvador (which I leave for in 5 days), and greater things to come. Wow! So much has happened in one morning. This morning has been a breath of fresh air. Heavenly air.

Lord, I thank You and praise You for the work You're doing and will continue to do in my heart and mind. Thank You for dying for me so that I might have life and have it more abundantly (John 10:10). Please help me realize more and more Your will for my life and teach me to walk it out. Take this life and make it Your own. In Your beautiful, precious and holy name, Jesus, Amen!

(June 6, 2002)

Today I went walking with some friends. One of them was saying how she thinks people should be free to have their own opinions about what's right and wrong. She went on to say that something may seem wrong to one person, but not to the next. I told my her that the thing I really like about where I am in my walk of faith is that I don't have to worry about what's right or wrong, or what's the best thing. I said that God, who created us and is all knowing, knows what's best for us. So, if I'm ever questioning whether something is right or wrong, all I have to do is look in God's Word, because the Word is good for testing (2 Timothy 3:16-17). That takes so much pressure off of me. Though God's Word might be really hard to follow sometimes, we can have peace because He knows what's best, and in the end, we will be happy that we chose to obey Him (Matthew 6:8).

I know from personal experience that it can be *very* hard (especially at first) to "live by faith, not by sight," and that it probably won't be an overnight change (2 Corinthians 5:7). But

God does help us change as we put our trust in Him. Since I've given my heart to the Lord (which was a year ago in two days!), God has been faithfully helping me to grow in my faith, pruning the bad things out of my life, and replacing them with His good things. And I am *so* grateful. I know that I have a long way to go, but I am on my way and that's what counts. I can honestly say that life with God is *so* much better than life without Him, even though it is difficult sometimes.

Questions:

1. Are there any new healthy habits you are having a hard time forming, or old habits you are having a hard time breaking right now? What is your plan to change this for the better?

2. How can someone know they are "born again"? Include Scripture references.

3. Write down your understanding of what it means to be a Christian.

4. What does the cross symbolize? Hint: Luke 9:23

5. Why is it dangerous for people to decide on their own what is right and wrong instead of seeking God's wisdom?

6. What did you learn about God in this chapter?

Chapter 6

Well, my mission trip to El Salvador was amazing! I felt the Holy Spirit with me in a powerful way, giving me grace to do God's work. So many things that would normally have been difficult for me were not, and so many things that I would have normally worried about or been afraid of didn't affect me. Don't get me wrong, it was hard work. Every day I needed to lay myself down before the Lord, surrender my will, and depend on Him. It really helped to be with a group of people who were passionate about Jesus and who were focused on the same mission directives. I felt so free and alive. Here are some excerpts from my journal while on this trip:

(June 11, 2002)

I'm in El Salvador! On the plane ride over I read a few chapters in the book of Joshua. Joshua was such an amazing warrior for God! I've been reading a lot lately about people in the Bible who lived so big for God, and it's inspired me even more to live big for God myself.

Lord, I pray that you will help me stay focused on You and passionately follow You.

Teach me how to surrender my all to You. I want to live big for You just like all of the people I've been reading about in the Bible.

(June 13, 2002)

We had five programs today! It made for a long day, but I have nothing to complain about. I have felt God with me in such a strong way. I haven't really been sick since I've been here. The most I've had is a headache. I've had great energy, and God has really been helping me keep my focus too.

Konan, the district youth director of Ohio, spoke to us for a little bit before we left for mission today. He talked about how God won't use us to do something mighty in public until we let Him do something mighty in private first. Then he talked about fighting the "lions" in our lives. He emphasized how we shouldn't only go so far as to fight them, then give up when it gets really hard; but that we need to be determined to fight them until we kill them. He said we'll probably always have lions in our lives that we need to fight, which means we need to continually build ourselves up in Christ so that we have the strength to keep fighting (Ephesians 6:10-20). By lions, he meant the things in our lives that are keeping us from completely trusting God and living a surrendered, holy, and righteous life before Him. Konan also said that our lions can come in all shapes and sizes, and that if we keep ignoring them, they will just get bigger, stronger, and harder to fight.

(June 14, 2002)

After our third program today, we went to a church service at the local Assemblies of God Church, and *man,* did those people know how to praise the Lord. When their worship band got up on stage, they played and sang their hearts out. During the second song, several of us gathered towards the front and started jumping up and down. It was so uplifting and inspiring. After the local worship band finished, the local pastor shared a short message, then our worship band got up and played. I loved the fact that the nationals of El Salvador knew some of the same worship songs as us, except they sang them in their own language. After we finished with worship, one of the pastors from our team shared a message. He talked about the importance of totally surrendering ourselves to God. He said that God wants to use us and He has a divine plan for all of our lives, but before He will begin to reveal that plan to us, we need to surrender our hearts and lives to Jesus—in others words, be born again. After he said this, he invited anyone who wanted to surrender their hearts and lives to Jesus for the first time to the front of the stage. Then he gave a second invitation for anyone who wanted the Lord to fill them up with more of Himself, a fresh baptism in the Spirit, if you will.

Our team prayed for the people who went up front. It was incredible! As soon as I laid my hands on someone to pray for them, the Lord would lay a specific thing on my heart to pray for. For some people it was a fresh filling of the Holy Spirit. For some, deliverance from strongholds. For others, I was just overcome with thankfulness for the joy I could sense that God was filling them with and the courage He was giving them to be a light in the darkness. I loved it!

(June 15, 2002)

After dinner today, we went to a church service at the church where we're staying. It was *really* awesome! The local pastor read quite a few scriptures about the end times. It was very powerful. Then the local band played some more songs. During the whole service, the Lord was really touching my heart, but it wasn't until the last few songs that I was really moved and couldn't hold back the tears. I just think it's so incredible to go to a place where you don't know anybody and you're able to worship God together in unity. I've been filled with such a sense of unity since I've been here. It makes me think about when we'll all be in heaven someday praising God together (Revelation 5:11-14).

(June 19, 2002)

Today was our last day of ministry in El Salvador, and it went really well. Before we left for mission, we all met together for a time of prayer and Biblical instruction. Our team leaders spoke to us about giving our all today. After they finished sharing, I felt the Holy Spirit stirring inside of me, creating in me the need to say something. He was reminding me how horrible it is to be lost and to not know about the hope we can have in Jesus, and the richness of God's love. I told everyone how important it is for us to share the love of Christ, and how important it is for us to give of ourselves so that others may share in the joy that we've found.

I believe that until we allow Christ to come into our hearts, we will always feel like we're missing something. So many people try to fill this gap with things like wealth, fame, relationships, media, food, alcohol, drugs, and more—only to be let down. This can be a vicious cycle. It is only when we completely surrender our hearts and lives to Jesus, stand on God's Word, and truly receive His unconditional love for us that this cycle can be broken. It might take some time, but as we continue to put our trust in Jesus the strongholds in our lives *will* be broken. I still struggle trusting Jesus in some areas. I suppose I always will. I am learning that I need to put my trust in Jesus everyday and every hour. I don't feel so overwhelmed when I focus on taking it one day at a time. It makes me incredibly thankful for God's amazing grace. It gives me great peace to know that if I mess up, all I have to do is lay my failure at the foot of the cross and my slate will be wiped clean.

My heart is to share Jesus with those who don't know Him and with believers who have become complacent in their walks with Christ, not in any particular part of the world. I feel like Jesus will lead me to a lot of different places.

Lord, let Your love burn like a fire in my soul and use me to spread that fire to the world.

In Your precious and holy name, Jesus. Amen.

Questions:

1. What makes you feel/come alive?

2. What do the lions in your life look like? (Addictions, fears, etc.)

3. Read Revelation 5:11-14. How does this passage make you feel?

4. What do you think is the best way to be an effective witness for Jesus, and whose job is it?

5. Write down the definition of "complacent." Now be honest and ask yourself if this describes your relationship with Jesus. If yes, then pray and ask God how you can change this.

Chapter 7

(July 22, 2002)

I have so much to write about. I want to talk about a very special day, not last Sunday, but the Sunday before. I went to the church I grew up in, then I stopped by the Assemblies of God Church, just in time to catch the last five minutes of the sermon. They had a guest speaker who was talking about seeing God's power at work in our lives. He finished by inviting anyone who wanted to see God's mighty power at work in their lives to come to the front and pray. Well, that was me! When I got to the front, I got down on my knees and prayed hard. I want *everything* God has for me! Well, of course God heard my prayer, and this time He was quick to answer.

That night I got into a conversation with a man at the Ohio Renaissance Festival. He claimed to be an atheist—to not believe in God. He was very intellectual, and we talked for a while. He asked me a lot of questions, and quite a few of them began with, "Why?" I was able to give some compelling answers, but I didn't have all the answers he was looking for. My responses to the questions that were beyond my understanding at the time were simply, "I don't know," or, "I just do." These responses were good enough for me. I'm not sure they were good enough for him though. I hope so. I have to admit, I was surprised with myself. I stood firm in my faith without question. I know for a fact that the Holy Spirit was there with me, giving me the words to say and the courage to stand firm. In fact, I had never felt so confident and bold in the face of adversity in my life! I know it was nothing short of an answer to my recent prayer to see God's mighty power at work in my life. God is so faithful!

A big thing I got out of our conversation was that Jesus didn't ruin it for this man. Others who claimed to be Christ followers, but who were very poor examples, did. Sometimes Christians can be such bad examples of Christ. I am sometimes guilty of this myself and I hate it! It's so easy to have a Christ-like attitude one minute, and the complete opposite the next. I just have to trust that God will help me become more and more like Him as I seek after Him.

Lord, please help us who profess faith in You to be good examples of You. I also pray that You would help people who are still searching to not let Christian's shortcomings keep them from accepting You. Because people will never be perfect, but You are.

I had a dream about a week after I talked to the man at the Renaissance Festival. In the dream, I was working at a facility that helped those who couldn't help themselves: mostly young children who were physically and mentally challenged, and orphans. I worked with a man who I believed had no business being there. He had a very bad temper and I could tell he hated his job. In my dream, I was in a room watching over some young children, and I heard the man come storming down the hall. I closed my eyes, and I could see a young, helpless boy in the room next to me become tense with fear. The children in the room gathered close around me as my co-worker began to yell at the boy in the next room for no other reason except for the fact that he needed help doing things most other people could do on their own. He began to become violent with this poor, helpless boy. All I could do was try and calm the terrified children who were gathered around me.

Then all of a sudden it was quiet. After a few seconds, I heard a loud knocking on the door of the room I was in. I knew it was the angry man. I answered the door as calmly as I could, and the man said in a very angry and demanding tone, "I need to talk to you!" I told the children to stay where they were, and that I would be right back.

I followed the man down an empty hallway leading to a stairwell. He continued to lead me down the stairs. After a brief period of time, I told him that I wanted to go where there were other people around, but he insisted that I follow him. Finally, we stopped in a small open space at the end of the stairs and he turned towards me, staring furiously into my eyes. After a few moments of intense silence, he cried out, in a loud voice filled with anger and desperation, "Where is God?!" It shocked me to hear those words come out of his mouth, but by the look on his face, I could tell that he had thought long and hard about this question but hadn't come up with a satisfactory answer. I could tell that he was very bitter. He was mad at God, and mad at the world. My heart broke for him, and I couldn't feel anything but compassion for him.

He had obviously suffered a great deal, and his heart was so hardened from it that he could no longer see God. The moment that he asked the question, "Where is God?" I could tell that his heart began to soften. I began to explain to him how much God loved him. I told him about Jesus and what He did for him on the cross. As I was talking to him about Jesus, all of these people began to appear and gather around him and do everything in their power to take his focus off of me. I told him to not pay attention to them. That he needed to focus on me. The voices around kept getting louder, but I continued to tell him about how much God loves him and how he could be washed clean of his sin and start over. I told him that all he had to do was confess he was a sinner in need of saving and believe that Jesus died to save him from his sin and bring him into God's family. Together, surrounded by loud voices, I led him in prayer as he committed his life to Christ.

As soon as we finished praying, everyone else in the room who was so eagerly trying to take this man's focus off of me disappeared, all except one man. I remember seeing this man lean in to listen as the others yelled and screamed for the other man's attention. After everyone else disappeared, this man said to me, "I want what he has." This dream was so incredibly vivid. I get chills as I think about the desert of despair that I saw in this man's eyes when he asked me where God was, then the complete change of heart after he accepted Christ. I can't help but think that this man in my dream represented the man I spoke to at the Renaissance Festival that said he didn't believe in God, and also many other people who are struggling like him to see God amidst all of the evil and disappointment in this world.

Questions:

1. Have you come into contact with anyone who seems to have rejected Jesus because of the bad witness of Christians, or people who call themselves Christians but are not? How did you respond?

2. How do you think Jesus would respond to someone who has rejected Him because of how He was misrepresented by others?

3. Are you confident in knowing how to tell someone how to become a Christian and praying with them to commit their lives to Christ? If not, take the time now to pray, read Scripture, and write down what you would say to someone who asked you how they can become a Christian, and how you would lead them in committing their lives to Christ.

Chapter 8

(August 19, 2002)

I have *so* much to write about. First, I want to talk about the last youth group meeting I went to. There was a missionary there from Africa, and when he spoke, he really stressed the fact that Jesus is the only way to God (John 14:6). He said that God wants to engrave this truth on our hearts so that we can stand firm in our faith, no matter what. He also talked about how we need to bring our problems to Jesus instead of trying to deal with them on our own, because Jesus is the answer to all of our problems. Jesus alone can truly lift our burdens and give us real peace (Matthew 11:28-30; I Peter 5:7). He also said that if we feel angry with God, we shouldn't keep it bottled up inside. He gave some examples from the book of Psalms where David expressed his anger and frustration to God (Psalm 13:1-6, 22:1-6, 22-31, 42:9-11). Notice that after David voices his complaints and anger to God, he always follows it up with praise. This is a very important step that we need to take care not to leave out in our efforts to clear the air with God. It might take some time, but we mustn't get discouraged. We should keep pressing through until we get a break through. Sandie Freed says:

> Worship has always been a foundation for experiencing His divine presence, which so

> often leads to breakthrough and a release of His majestic power. It will Not be our traditions and old patterns of thinking that break open the floodgates. Floodgates open because we have fully surrendered our lives to Him and we trust Him. When He has a throne in our lives, He can fully rule and reign over our daily activities and our difficult situations. With His seated position in our lives, He promises to give us living water and this living water flows from His throne! Hallelujah! [3]

God is faithful. As Scripture says, "Anyone who believes in him will never be put to shame. For there is no difference between Jew and Gentile—the same Lord is Lord of all and richly blesses all who call on him" (Romans 10:11-12).

Bring Jesus Back Ministries

Now to write about something that has been a big part of my life since early March—Bring Jesus Back Ministries outreach event. As I was working the midnight shift at the Assisted Living Home, I felt a strong urge to begin planning an outreach event. I didn't exactly know where it was going to be, when it was going to take place, or who was going to be involved. All I knew was that the Lord had placed it on my heart to plan an event that would be focused on telling people about the importance of having a personal relationship with Him and using one's gifts and talents to bring Him glory.

Well I must say, it was quite an exciting journey planning the event. It involved many hours of searching through the Scriptures, taking notes, writing down ideas, and talking to people that might be able to help make this event a success. It was exciting to see everything come together. Pastor John, kids from the youth group I attend, people from the church I grew up in, and my family helped to make the event a success. Also, four local Christian bands came and played, someone rented out some really nice sound equipment and arranged for some staff members from a local music shop to come and run it, and a Bible printing company donated one hundred paperback New Testament Bibles. Approximately 170 people showed up!

After six months of preparation I couldn't help but have high expectations for the event, and through God's grace and goodness, my expectations were met and surpassed. Words cannot express the awe I felt as I saw, by the expression of love on each person's face, the awesome hand of God reach down and, for a moment in time, allow us to experience an undeniable connection with Him and with each other. It was so beautiful!

Questions:

1. Do you believe Jesus is the only way to receive eternal life? If yes, why? If no, why?

2. Make a list of some ways one could go about bringing their problems to Jesus and receiving help from Him.

3. Write the definition of "praise."

4. Has God been stirring in your heart to do any sort of outreach? If yes, write it down and get to work!

5. Pray and ask God to direct you to a person or people He wants you to reach out to.

James J. Gettel says:

> Ministering to others is especially important to our spiritual growth. A passionate and growing Christian needs a ministry to others. One of the wonders of our faith is that we discover even greater spiritual gifts by using our gifts (I Corinthians 14:12). Our faith does not just grow by what we think or believe, but by what we do and experience. By serving Jesus, we also come to see and know Jesus more… The keys for God's love to transform us are personal involvement and actually serving other people. The particular ministry that we are passionate about will depend on God's particular call to us based on where we are on our own spiritual journey. Mother Theresa reminded us "there are no great deeds, only small deeds done with great love." We each need to ask ourselves how we are intended to be instruments of God's love in the world.[4]

6. Are you aware of your specific gifts and talents? What are they? How are you doing at developing them and using them to glorify God?[5]

Chapter 9

(October 22, 2002)

I moved out of my parents' house about three weeks ago. I moved in with Christine (one of my massage instructors) and her family. I moved here in order to help her start a massage business and help out with her three young children. I like living here, they are a really nice family. My first weekend I was here was the weekend of my graduation from the American Institute of Massage Therapy! Woo hoo!

I must say, with all the changes in my life, there is one thing that remains the same: God's presence in my life. I've found that wherever I go and whatever I'm doing, He always helps me to find Him there.

Right now, I'm going through one of Beth Moore's Bible studies called *Breaking Free*. This morning's study was all about how, as believers, we are the righteousness of God in Christ, and that any thought we have about ourselves other than being a purified vessel, clothed in righteousness and shining with beauty, is a lie. This is amazing to me! Of course we are not perfect and we need to continue working toward holiness and learning to walk in the Spirit; but the moment we are born again, when God looks on us, He sees the image of His Son—pure, righteous, and beautiful. We are saved by grace, through faith, and this not of ourselves, but of God, through Christ Jesus our Lord (Ephesians 2:8). How amazing is this!! Ahhh! I want the whole world to know!

I want so badly to be used by God to share this good news with the world. I am not as consistent at doing this as I want to be, though. Sometimes I feel so empowered by God to be a light for Him, and I know that power comes when I diligently seek after Him. I just wish I always felt motivated to seek Him with such passion. It seems like I've been on an up-and-down roller coaster lately as far as my desire to seek after God is concerned. I hate this! I know that in this world I will face trials, and that some of those trials will be facing my own demons, struggles, and fears. I just hope and pray that these encounters will only make me stronger and draw me closer to the Lord instead of pushing me away.

(January 16, 2003)

I've been reading a book written by John Eldridge entitled *The Journey of Desire*, and it's *so* good! I haven't been able to put it down. It's helped to confirm some things God has already spoken to me. Some things are still vague, but I feel like I have enough to get started. It's also made me feel very unsettled about where I am. This, in turn, has caused me to really seek God regarding whether or not I'm supposed to stay here. I really want to make sure this unsettled feeling is from God because of the commitment I've made to Christine to help her out. I am praying for a clear confirmation on this subject.

(January 17, 2003)

Well, my confirmation came today! This morning Christine told me that she knows that there's something I need to do, and to not let her or her family hold me back. I was amazed, because I hadn't expressed any of my feelings of being unsettled to her or anyone else (except for God of course). This was a quick answer!

So, after some prayerful consideration, I've decided I'm going to move down to Columbus with my older sister Liz and work until next fall. Then I want to pursue a career as a movie actress. After that, or maybe even during that time, I want to focus on developing Bring Jesus Back Ministries.

Dear Lord, thank You for Your promise to never leave me or forsake me and thank You for helping me to continue to have a close personal relationship with You and continue to press forward with Your plans for me. Please help me to stay close to You and focused on Your plans for me as I make this new move. In Your precious and holy name, Jesus, Amen!

Questions:

1. What does it mean that we are "saved by grace through faith"? Refer to Romans chapters 1-8.

2. Make a list of your top three personal struggles. For example, "being led by your emotions."

3. What is the Bible's definition of "faith"? Refer to Hebrews chapter 11; James 2:14-26.

4. What do you feel that God is calling you to do with your life?

Chapter 10

(February 8, 2003)

There is *so* much to write about. A lot has happened in the past couple of weeks. I talked to Christine about my plans to move to Columbus with Liz. She told me that she and her family would really miss me but they were also excited for me. Moving was bitter-sweet. This is the farthest I've lived from home. I will really miss my family (all except Liz of course). I almost chickened out of moving to Columbus the day before I left, but my mom reminded me of how badly I had wanted to move there and about the great opportunities that awaited me there. *Thanks Mom!*

In the midst of moving, something else in my life has changed: my feelings for my boyfriend. We've been dating for about three months now. It doesn't make sense to me. I mean, I was so sure about him in the beginning. Sometimes I get so frustrated with myself because it seems like one moment I'm totally sure about someone, then the next moment I'm not so sure. I guess I just have to trust that God is in all of this. I *have* asked for His guidance after all. So maybe this is a sign that we just aren't meant for each other *(which is fine);* I just want to know one way or another.

So as far as living with my older sister Liz and her roommate—I like it a lot! Liz is usually pretty busy with work and school and other miscellaneous stuff. I told her that she's lucky she has stuff to do (I am still looking for a job). I've realized that I feel much better about myself when I have things to do, especially things having to do with being around people and being of some sort of service to them.

(February 13, 2003)

So, my boyfriend and I broke up. I'm not *too* heart broken. I guess I saw it coming. I know God is in control. If anything, I've learned not to rush into anything no matter how *right* it feels at the time.

I'm just sick of being a confused mess when it comes to guys! I know there has to be a perfect guy out there for me, just like I'm perfect for him; otherwise I wouldn't want it so badly. I know I just need to trust God, be patient, and let *Him* be enough for me. My relationship with the Lord is so beautiful. I want to be with someone who will bring out that beauty. I know that I need to grow in my relationship with the Lord first before I even think about pursuing any other serious relationships.

Questions:

1. Are you currently in a dating relationship that you feel is hindering your relationship with the Lord? If yes, why? And what were the circumstances and motives behind you entering into that relationship? Now pray and ask God if you should stay in this relationship. If no, then I would highly recommend ending it. If yes, ask God what changes you need to make to draw closer to Him.

2. From where do you get your feelings of value and self-worth from?

Chapter 11

(April 23, 2003)

It's 3:25 a.m. I've been awake for about two hours now. I woke up around 1:30 a.m. to the sound of Liz quietly whispering through my bedroom door asking me if she could come in. She sounded really upset, so of course I said yes. She came in and sat down on the floor next to my bed (which consists of two mattresses on the floor) and buried her face in my knees trying to hold back her tears. After a few minutes of trying to collect herself, she told me that she had just spent the last six hours with one of her best friends who confessed to her that she had recently tried to commit suicide.

My heart sank when she told me this. I know her friend. I actually gave her a massage shortly after I moved to Columbus. We even had a good conversation about God and faith. I would have never guessed she was so low. Liz told me something very encouraging during our conversation tonight, which I know seems odd to say in light of the situation. She said that her friend mentioned to her tonight how much a really spiritual, faith filled person can help in desperate situations, and that they both saw me as such. I felt very humbled. This really encouraged me because I've been trying really hard to grow in my faith and "let my light shine" (Matthew 5:16). God is so faithful! This situation is actually one of many ways that God has been bringing me encouragement lately and letting me know that I'm doing a good job.

Here are just a few more examples:

So, a couple of weeks ago, while I was working at Q Salon and Day Spa (where I'm employed as a massage therapist), I got into a spiritual conversation with a lady I was giving a massage to. She's a Christian, and we had a wonderful conversation in which I shared my testimony, how in love with God I am, and about how faithful He has been to me. When the massage came to an end, she very sincerely thanked me for sharing with her. Then she said something that really blessed me, "Ya know, I came to get a massage, but I got an angel instead." If she only knew how much those words meant to me. When she told me that, it was like God was speaking through her, telling me I was on the right track and to keep up the good work. Then, only a couple of days later while I was working at Olive Garden (where I am employed part-time as a waitress), a woman at one of my tables asked me, "Do you go to church?" I proudly and enthusiastically said, "Yes I do!" Then she said, "You just seem like somebody that would go to church." She then explained to me that her and her husband were born again believers. As she told me this, I couldn't help but express my joy and excitement and also gratitude for her words of encouragement. It really blessed me that she could recognize the Spirit of God in me. I want so badly for Jesus to shine really brightly through me.

In other exciting news, I went to the Ohio Assemblies of God youth conference last weekend in Columbus. A while back, Pastor John had asked me if I would be interested in being a chaperone for the youth on the trip since I now live in Columbus. Of course I said "yes." Well, let me tell you, I am *so* glad I did. It was there that I learned about a young adults discipleship school called "Master's Commission" which exactly fits the description of the kind of school that I've recently been having a strong desire to attend. I mean, I enjoy working as a massage therapist, and sort of as a waitress, but I'm having a stronger and stronger desire to grow in Biblical knowledge and get more involved in ministry. Anyway, after one of the main sessions ended, I wanted to let the main speaker know how inspired I was by his message, but the line to his table was so long that I ended up speaking to his director of scheduling instead. I asked him what one would have to do to be able to go around and speak at events like this. He pretty much said that you have to have a passion for it and be called to it by God. Well, I know I have both of those things. He then told me about Master's Commission, which is where he went to train for ministry. He directed me to a table where a Master's Commission school from around the area was handing out information. I went and talked to them after lunch. They were really nice. I ended up taking one of their brochures. I've read through it and, like I said earlier, it's exactly the kind of school I've been wanting to attend. It's either a one or two year program, and some schools even offer a third year. The first year is all about building a solid foundation in your faith. The second and third year are more for people who want to go into full-time ministry, though it will benefit anyone. This particular school starts in September, which is four months from now. I really want to go! I know it's God's will for me to attend. I'm just not sure if I'm supposed to go there now or if I need to wait. There is also something else that's caught my eye recently. I was watching Pastor John Hagee on TV, and he was advertising a new Christian movie that's just come out in association with Cloud Ten Pictures, which is a Christian based motion picture company. When I saw this, it really stirred up my desire to act in movies. So that's something else I'm considering as a next step.

Well, it's 4:33 a.m. and my alarm is set for 7:30 a.m. I hope I'm not too tired tomorrow. I have to work, then later on my best friend Cathy and I are supposed to hang out. We don't get a chance to hang out very often. I've been pretty busy with both jobs and she has school and a job as well.

(April 29, 2003)

So I decided to attend Reality Master's Commission this September! The director, assistant director, and some other representatives from the school came to the Assembly of God Church in my hometown last Sunday to make a presentation about their school. I made it a point to go and hear what they had to say. I felt that hearing their presentation would help me come to a definite decision about whether I should attend this September or wait. Well, when I brought it to God in prayer during the service and specifically asked if I was supposed to attend this September, I clearly heard the word "destiny." I knew this meant that attending Reality Master's Commission this September was part of His plan for me. I talked to the director and the assistant director after the meeting and turned in my application. After our conversation (which felt like a mini interview) I felt very confident that I would be accepted.

Dear God, I just want to let you know that I'm so excited to spend nine months with You, running after You like never before. I'm excited for what You're going to teach me and what You're going to do in and through me, and how my relationship with You is going to grow deeper and deeper. Thank You, thank You, thank You!

Questions:

1. How do you feel like you're doing at "letting your light shine" for Jesus? How can you improve?

2. Do you have a clear picture of what God is calling you to do? If so, write it down. If you don't have a clear picture, but you have some of the picture, write down what you do know.

3. What are you currently doing to be be discipled, grow in your gifting's, and work toward what you know of God's plan for you? Do you feel like this discipleship has been effective in drawing you closer to Jesus? Do you want something more? If so, pray and ask God to guide you as to what, where, when, how and with whom. Right now, write down anything you feel God is speaking to you in response to this prayer.

Chapter 12

(June 20, 2003)

Recently God has been introducing me to the gift of prophecy. Pastor, author, and speaker John Piper defines prophecy as this:

1. A regulated message or report in human words.
2. Usually made to the gathered believers.
3. Based on a spontaneous, personal revelation from the Holy Spirit.
4. For the purpose of edification, encouragement, consolation, conviction, or guidance.
5. But not necessarily free from a mixture of human error, and thus needing assessment.
6. On the basis of the apostolic (Biblical) teaching.
7. Mature spiritual wisdom.[6]

So, about a week ago, a guy I work with at the Olive Garden invited me to a small group meeting that he attends with some people from his church. I really enjoyed it. I got along particularly well with a guy there named Scott.

Scott was telling me about a church that he occasionally attends in Peebles, Ohio, called Shepherd's Heart, and about how much he *really* loves it. I actually went with him to visit the church this past Sunday morning and I am so glad I did!

I was very inspired and encouraged by what the pastor had to say, but that's not the best part. After the service was over, Scott introduced me to the pastor. His name is David and he has a very strong prophetic gifting. Scott asked him if he and one of the other men there, Tom (who also has a strong prophetic gifting), would pray for me. Of course they were more than happy to oblige. I wasn't prepared for what happened next.

When they prayed for me, they spoke for God using first person phrases like "my daughter." I had never been prayed for in this way. It was truly a transcendent experience. God spoke through them, saying, "I am getting ready to bring balance into your life. No more will you be tossed back and forth by the waves. I am going to place your feet on solid ground. I will build your confidence and cause you to rise up and soar like the eagles. You will experience new things and, in the process, grow closer to Me." This is everything I've been feeling and desiring deep in my heart! It was a total confirmation that I am on the right track. I believe that God will use Master's Commission to accomplish much of what God promised in that prayer, or at least lay the foundation. I'm *so* excited! This whole experience has strengthened my faith and stirred in me a desire to draw even closer to God and learn more about the gift of prophecy. I want to be able to hear God's voice like they do for myself and for other people. It actually says in 1 Corinthians 14:1 that we should "Follow the way of love and eagerly desire gifts of the Spirit, especially prophecy."

(July 6, 2003)

God to me:

> I am doing a great work in you. Do not compromise My ways (by accepting standards that are lower than My best). There is so much that I want to give you. I am raising up a generation of mighty

> warriors. They shall not run in fear, they shall run by faith, and you are one of those warriors. I'm going to do the things that I said I would do.

God, I want everything You have for me. I'm not afraid of the commitment, because I know You will help me fulfill it and that it will be worth it. You are worth it! I don't just want to be a hearer of the Word. I want to be a doer. I don't just want a moment. I want a lifetime. Lord, help me to see my trials and tribulations through Your eyes. They are nothing compared to the joy of being with You!

(July 24, 2003)

Lord, You've spoken to me through one of Your prophets that You will bring me through a season where You will teach me my identity in You, and what it means to walk by faith. You have made me aware that You are bringing me through a time of refinement. You have revealed that You have a lot to teach me. I want all that You have for me Lord! Whatever it takes. I know that this can be a dangerous prayer, but I also know that Your plans are to prosper me and not to harm me, to give me a hope and a future—so I don't need to be afraid (Jeremiah 29:11). Lord help me not to count my burdens but to count my blessings. My hope is in You. Show me your ways. I pray for knowledge and wisdom, passion and purpose, strength and courage, conviction and good character; pretty much, just help me to put You first.

Questions:

1. Have you ever been prophetically prayed for? If so, describe your experience. What did God speak to you?

2. Write the definition of "refinement" and describe how it applies to Christianity.

3. What did you learn about God in this chapter?

Chapter 13

(August 14, 2003)

Today was a good day. It started off by picking Liz up from the airport. She just got back from the National Flute Convention in Las Vegas, and from visiting our brother Greg in Arizona. I felt really bad for her because, on top of being really tired, she had a very busy day planned. She had to go to a class, teach a lesson, go to work, *and* catch up on school work. After we got home and she finished getting ready for her busy day, she asked me where her car keys were. I looked where I thought I had put them and they weren't there! I frantically searched everywhere else I could think of and they were nowhere to be found, so I let her take my car to school.

She got back at 11:30 a.m. and I still hadn't been able to find her keys. So, with all the other stuff she needed to figure out how to take care of today (which was really stressing her out) not being able to find her keys just topped it off. I felt really bad. She ended up canceling her teaching lesson, and said if she couldn't find her keys by 5 p.m. that she would just call off work as well. I had to be at work at 12 p.m., so I couldn't help her look anymore. Well, she wasn't able to find her keys and ended up having to call off work. She later told me that she slept from 1 p.m. to 5:30 p.m., which I know she desperately needed.

Now here's the real kicker. I had a one hour break from 6 to 7 p.m. and I decided to run home and get some dinner. Well, on my way home I was praying and asking God to help me find Liz's car keys. I then got a very clear image in my mind of my black bag, and I saw Liz's keys in one of the side pockets. As soon as I got home, I went right upstairs and checked the side pocket of my black bag and, *sure enough,* her keys were there! I walked downstairs with her keys behind my back and said, "Ya know how I couldn't find your keys earlier..." I couldn't contain my laughter any longer and I removed her keys from behind my back. Liz quickly raised her left hand towards me and said, "Give me those!" I sat down on the couch beside her and handed over her keys. In-between laughter she said, "I ought to smack you!" We had a good laugh. In fact, we laughed so hard that at times it was hard to catch our breath. It was really refreshing.

So this is my conclusion: God didn't allow us to find the keys when we wanted to because He had a better plan. Liz got some much needed rest and was able to catch up on some school work. It was very encouraging to me, because for the past couple of days I haven't been very confident in my ability to hear God's voice clearly like I desperately want to. But today, I realized that God is still in control and is faithful to be right on time, which isn't always our timing. I've never had such a clear picture either, which of course I was super excited about.

Questions:

1. Think of a time that something didn't happen when you wanted it to, but afterward you realized that God had a better plan. Write down a brief description.

2. How are you doing at trusting in God's timing? For example, do you get really upset and worried when things don't happen when you want them to, or do you have peace that God is in control?

Chapter 14

(August 22, 2003)

So, for the past four months I have been working hard to save money and prepare my heart and mind to attend Reality Master's Commission. In the process, the Holy Spirit has been making me aware of things about myself that I need to work on. For example, sometimes it's hard for me to be satisfied just being still with God. I've realized that hanging out with people is a *big* thing for me. I'm sure I would be able to hear from God more clearly if I would just learn how to let Him be enough for me. I realized today that so many of us are so in tune with the desires of our flesh much more than we are with the desires of the Spirit of God. I would like it to be the other way around for me.

I've already said goodbye to Scott, who became my boyfriend a couple of months ago. He is so passionate about God and has been a real encouragement to me in my journey of faith. I am thankful that our paths have crossed. I'm not sure what the future holds for us. Master's Commission students aren't allowed to date anyone during their first year, so that's why I had to say goodbye to him. We plan on continuing our relationship after Master's Commission, if it be God's will. I'm not worried about it. I'm just really excited to spend nine months focusing solely on my relationship with God.

(September 3, 2003)

Well, I'm here! I am officially a Reality Master's Commission student! Wow! I am so excited to be here! After orientation yesterday, we moved into our host family houses. My host family seems super nice. As part of our orientation, we had a service at church, during which I felt God's presence *so* strong. After worship, Pastor Andy (the director) spoke. He focused on the importance of building a solid foundation in our faith, and how building a solid foundation is going to take dedication, discipline, attention, and passion. He also talked about change and how, when we give something up like a bad habit, it's important to replace it with something better so we don't go back to our old ways. He talked about how we need to allow God to fill these empty voids in us. I hope to apply this wisdom to different areas in my life that God has brought to my attention that *well*, need attention.

I want so badly to become more connected with God and grow in my faith. I've tasted and seen that the Lord is good (Psalm 34:8; 1 Peter 2:2-3). I've heard over and over that Jesus is enough (Philippians 4:19). I want my life to be a testimony to this fact.

I've met so many people, myself included, that have tried so many things other than Jesus to bring satisfaction; and all of these things have never *really* satisfied, they've only left residual feelings of emptiness, loneliness, bitterness and hopelessness. It says in the Word that as Christians we must stop living to please ourselves, and start living to please God (1 Thessalonians 4:1-11). This can be incredibly hard sometimes. It takes a lot of faith. I know from personal experience that a life of faith can be very challenging and scary, but at the same time, it is so and worth it!

As Christians, we are supposed to be ambassadors of Christ (2 Corinthians 5:20). I have learned that the more we surrender our hearts and lives to Christ and let His unconditional love penetrate the deepest recesses of our souls, the more effective we will be at bringing Christ to the world. I remember someone at

Church saying that the world is waiting for us to get a hold of Christ. What a powerful statement, as the world becomes more and more infested with sin and the cries for help become louder and louder. I've also learned that our choices are an outward expression of whatever is inside of us. This means that God, and His great love for us through the cross of Christ, needs to become a lot more present in the hearts and minds of a lot more people, myself included. Let us who profess to be Christians, run hard after Him, so that God can use us to shine His light in this dark world (Matthew 5:14-16; John 1:1-4).

Lord, please help me to stay focused on You. I came here to draw closer to You, to learn more of who I am in You, to grow in wisdom, to be more sensitive to Your Spirit, to gain experience and skills for life and ministry. I pray for the courage and strength to keep taking steps of faith.

Questions:

1. List some things that distract you from spending time with God.

2. Which would you say you are mostly allowing to lead you, your flesh or the Spirit? If you've answered "your flesh", then I would highly recommend seeking the baptism of the Holy Spirit. If you have already received the baptism of the Holy Spirit, then seek it fresh and new. We cannot live a Spirit-led life in our own strength. We need the help of the Holy Spirit. This comes through the reading of the Word and through the Spirit's baptism. I am convinced that you cannot separate the two (Acts 2).

3. Are there any bad habits that you've recently (or not so recently) given up, and what have you replaced them with that will help you grow closer to God? If you haven't replaced them with anything to help you grow closer to God, then pray now and ask God what He would have you institute into your life that would be the most effective in drawing you closer to Him. Now, pray for strength to be consistent and not fall back into old bad habits. If you have fallen back, repent now and make a fresh commitment to trust God with these things again.

4. On a scale of 1 to 10, 10 being completely surrendered, how surrendered do you feel you are in your heart and mind to following God's will for your life?

Chapter 15

(September 11, 2003)

Dear God, I need You! I know You have led me here to Reality Master's Commission, and for that I am so grateful. You are so faithful! Lord, You know I want everything You have for me and You know all the things that hinder me. Help me become more aware of these things and lay them down so that I can have more of You.

God to me:

> My child, be encouraged. What are those things compared to Me? I am for you. I believe in you. I will help you. I am so proud of you. I want you to know that I am so filled with joy when I see who you have become and I am excited for you to see what else I have for you. Keep seeking Me. Draw near to Me, and I will draw near to you (James 4:8). Praise Me. Remember My faithfulness. This will help you.

(September 14, 2003)

God to me:

> My child, My beautiful, beautiful child; take hold of Me. Let go of your past. You are a new creation (2 Corinthians 5:17). I've given you My blessing, and I am eagerly waiting for you to fully take hold of it. Take hold of My truths. Believe you are forgiven. Believe you are a new creation. Believe I am working in you. Keep pressing on. Be encouraged. You are doing a good job. I see your heart. I know you love Me. You are growing up spiritually. You are.

(September 16, 2003)

God to me:

> My child, stand on My promises. They are for you. Just reach up and grab them. Take off the garments of "second best" and "not enough." Throw them off and put on your new clothes. You are a leader. You can do it. You have My blessing.

(September 18, 2003)

Dear Jesus, thank You for speaking so clearly to me, and thank You for all the people You have brought into my life to minister to me and help me grow. You have never let me down. You are so wonderful. I don't want to live just an "okay" life for You. I want to live big for You. Lord, I pray that You continue to confirm Your plans for my life, so that I know beyond all doubt the steps that You want me to take.

God to me:

> My sweet, sweet child, you bring Me so much joy. I love your heart. It is so full of desire. Tell Me, how much more do I bless those who hunger and thirst for righteousness (Matthew 5:6)? Trust Me. I know the plans I have for you (Jeremiah 29:11). I will order your steps. Your mind is still dark in areas, that is why you sometimes feel depressed. You really need to read My Word more and try harder to see yourself how I see you. You know I think you are beautiful. Please set your sights on things above. I love you.

(October 1, 2003)

Dear Lord, I pray that You would broaden my horizons that I might see more of the big picture. I pray that I would consider my present struggles as nothing compared to the future glory that is waiting to be revealed (Romans 8:18). The Word says that for the joy set before You, You endured the cross (Hebrews 12:2). Oh, that I might set my sights upon that same joy. That I might carry my cross with more readiness and passion. Lord, You are greater than I can even comprehend, and You deserve all glory and honor and praise.

(October 11, 2003)

I am struggling Lord.

God to me:

> Stop trying to do things in your own strength. It is not for you to carry such a heavy burden. Return to Me and I will return to you (Zechariah 1:3). Raise your eyes up to the heavens. Where does

> your strength come from (Psalm 121:1-2)? I want you to lift people up to My throne. Tell them how much I love them. Remind yourself how much I love you, and let that be enough.

(October 21, 2003)

God, the more I learn about You, the more I fall in love with You. I am understanding this whole "free will" thing more. I know that it's my responsibility to choose to walk by faith. I know You can't make this decision for me. It's up to me to choose to pick up my cross daily and follow You (Mark 8:34). You can help steer me in the right direction, but, in the end, it's my choice to choose Your path. Oh Lord, You know that I want more than anything to follow after You and be obedient to Your will for my life. I say this, being well aware that I do have an adversary whose mission it is to steal, kill, and destroy; but You have come that I may have life, and have it the full (John 10:10). So, I commit myself and my ways to You, fresh and new. I need You Lord. I know this full well. Amen.

(November 16, 2003)

God to me:

> I have given you everything you need to live a righteous life (Ephesians 1:3). Let go of what you need to let go of, and hold onto what you need to hold onto. Hold onto Me. Stay surrendered to Me. Never look away from Me. Hold My words close to your heart and you will have peace and know what to do when you are supposed to do it (Romans 12:1-2).

Lord, I'm trying my best to trust You and hold onto the promise that You work everything out for the good of those who love You (Romans

8:28). Thank You for cultivating my heart. Thank You for pulling the lies out and making sure Your truth is growing well and producing fruit. Thank You for being so gentle and patient with me. I desire with all my being to be used by You for Your glory. I know my life is not my own (1 Corinthians 6:19-20; Psalm 100:3). Let Your will be done in my life. Less of me and more of You.

(November 22, 2003)

God to me:

> My child, take off the garment of self doubt and put on the garment of praise. You can trust Me. Keep repeating that over and over until you really believe it. I am the Vine and you are the branch, apart from Me you can do nothing (John 15:5). Abide in Me. Come and dine with Me. Enter into My presence and be satisfied. Do not continue to stand far off. Draw near to Me. Yield and commit your whole self to Me. There is a great work that needs to be done and a great battle. Seek Me diligently. I have a great work for you to do.

(December 4, 2003)

God, You are doing so many awesome things in my life right now. Thank You! Thank You for teaching me to trust You more.

Questions:

1. Do you believe that there is anything you can do that will cause God to stop loving you?

2. Now look up 1 Corinthians 13:4-7 and write it down. Meditate on the fact that this is how God feels about *you*, and know that He will never stop loving you, no matter what.

3. Ask God what He sees when He looks at you? Write down what He says.

Chapter 16

(January 3, 2004)

It's hard for me to put into words or express my gratitude for what God has done and is doing inside of me right now. He has faithfully been putting the broken pieces of my soul back together and making me whole. I know my biggest problem has been with myself, specifically being insecure and having low self-esteem. Now instead of always looking at myself through my own eyes (which I realize have been tainted by a worldly view), God has been helping me to look at myself through His eyes. My eyes can be very judgmental and unmerciful, but God's eyes are very merciful and gracious and loving.

In other news, recently, there have been quite a few times that I have struggled with being mad at God. I feel like this is the first time I have dealt with being angry at God, at least to this degree. I guess you could say it was like our first real fight, all coming from me of course. I hated that I even felt this way toward God. I felt ashamed, and I wanted to pretend like it just never happened. I knew God wanted me to talk to Him about it, though, and not just ignore it. When I went to Him and apologized, He didn't get mad at me and start accusing me (like some people tend to do with each other), even though it *was* my fault. He was very patient, and He gently revealed to me that I was giving into my carnal nature, which I've noticed tends to flare up when I go home. Basically,

I wanted what I wanted, I wasn't getting it, and I was mad. It sounds so ugly now that I've verbalized it. It didn't feel so wrong in the moment, though. I've learned that this is what happens when we obey our carnal nature. We become deceived into thinking our actions are justified or right. The key word here is "deceived." This is why it's so important to bring our sin into the light and confess it as soon as we become aware of it. When it's left in the darkness it will only grow and gain a stronger hold on us. In turn, it will be harder for us to break free from our sin, and this is exactly what the devil wants. When sin is brought into the light it is seen for what it is— deceptive, ugly and dangerous. Satan has deceived so many people in the world, myself included at times. He *is* known as the "Father of Lies" after all (John 8:44). I'm convinced that if we could always see sin for what it is, we wouldn't even have a hint of temptation to give in to it, and we would run as fast as we could in the opposite direction. Sometimes it's easy to forget the truth of this principle though. That's why we have to constantly read the Word, which shines a light on sin in our lives and helps us stay connected with God: He's the Light and is worthy of *all* our praise and worship.

When God revealed all of this to me, my anger quickly subsided. I'm so glad I talked to Him right away about it instead of bottling it up inside and not dealing with it, which is something I've realized is a tendency of mine. I've learned that sin that isn't dealt with right away, specifically in close relationships, can cause a lot of tension and distance. If left for too long, the result can be a severing of the relationship. I obviously do *not* want this to happen between me and God (or anyone else for that matter)! Romans 12:18 says, "If it is possible, as far as it depends on you, live at peace with everyone." I've learned that we can only control our *own* actions. If a relationships ends, we can have peace if we know we've done our part, and I believe God will let you know if you've done your part if you are truly desiring to please Him. Like I said earlier, Satan's mission is to separate us from God and each other, but it's God's heart and mission for us to be in perfect union with Him and with each other. This story is a good example of this beautiful truth.

I'm learning to be thankful for times like these because, even though they tend to be uncomfortable and difficult at the time (because my flesh doesn't want to submit to the Spirit of God), I know it is God helping me to grow up spiritually— which is what I *really* want.

God has shown me a special prayer to pray during these times when anger and discouragement try to take hold: "I give this to You Lord, and thank You that it will turn it out for Your glory." It never fails. Every time that I've prayed this prayer and given my anger and sadness to God, He blesses me and reveals more of Himself to me.

Questions:

1. How good do you think you are at consistently looking at yourself through God's eyes?

2. Is there anything you are currently mad at God about? If not, can you think of a time (or a few times) that you were mad at God? What were you mad about, and how did you come to a resolution?

3. Is there anyone in your life that you are mad at, or that you are struggling to forgive, or that you know is mad with you? If so, why?

4. Write down the definition of "forgiveness."

5. Research Bible verses, especially those in the New Testament, that talk about forgiveness. Write down at least three.

Chapter 17

(March 5, 2004)

We have been in Romania for a little over a week now. So far we've had several children's programs, visited a women's prison, and hosted some lovely tea parties. The tea party we hosted at the church tonight was especially good. The women at the church here are very passionate about God. I felt God's presence so strong as the women were singing and praying.

God is really moving in this country, especially since the fall of communism. Jan (one of our missionary leaders) said that since communism fell in 1989, the number of pentecostal churches in Romania grew from 700 to now 2,540! It is so amazing to see how God moves in different parts of the world. It is a stark reminder to me that God loves everyone and wants all to be saved and come to a knowledge of the truth (1 Timothy 2:1-4). It also makes me feel a very strong sense of connection to the Body of Christ throughout the world. (1 Corinthians 12:13; Ephesians 6:18). We are all in this together (Romans 12:5; Ephesians 6:18).

The first three or four days here were kind of hard for me. I think I was missing our regular routine in Master's of having a set time to pray in the morning, and from there going to class. Going to class is one of my favorite things to do right now. I am *so* hungry for knowledge. I really enjoy just sitting and listening to people teach about the Bible, prayer, faith, and ministry, etc. Something I have really enjoyed here is listening to our host missionaries talk about what it's like being a missionary, some of their experiences on the mission field, and the lessons they've learned as a result.

(March 10, 2004)

Dear Lord, thank You for opening my eyes and guiding my steps. I love You so much. Thank You for always believing in me.

God to me:

> My child, I know what I want you to do is more important to you than what you want to do and, because you have delighted yourself in Me, you won't miss Me. The times when you struggle are the times you stray from Me. Remain in Me. I am the vine (John 15:5). I will take care of you. You are doing so good. I am so proud of you. You've come a long way. You know that your place is in Me. I will always be there for you. I will wait for you. You won't miss out. Deal with whatever you need to deal with. Go back and rebuild the ruins.

How do I rebuild?

God to me:

> Replace the lies with My Truth.

(March 21, 2004)

Dear Lord, Thank You for continuing to set me free from fears that have been holding me back. Thank You for taking care of me and giving me what I need to continue to move forward in You.

God to me:

> My sweet child, there are going to be times when your eyes are going to have a hard time believing what they see, but believe it. Believe it! I am about to do something in these days that will make people question if what they are living for is worth it. I am bringing those things that have been lurking in the darkness into the light.

(April 2, 2004)

Lord, I know You are doing awesome things in me. Even though I don't see everything or understand, I know You are. Thank You for giving me a stronger faith and blessing me with a real, sustaining hope. Thank You for making the holes in my soul smaller and smaller. It definitely feels more natural to be with You than to be without You. Thank You for taking care of me and keeping me like You said You would.

(April 6, 2004)

God has been blessing me *so* much lately! Recently, my car overheated and, as a result, major damage was done to the engine and other things. It was to the point where the mechanics that looked at it didn't know if it was even worth fixing. But Butch, one of my home openers, asked around and found a guy from church who owns an auto shop who fixed it for under $300. I think the original estimate to get it fixed was $2,200! The church here has definitely been like a family to me. My home openers have been especially amazing! They have helped me out *so* much, shown me so much generosity, and have been a great source of encouragement to me. Also, a couple of weeks ago, we had a girl's night for The Jar (the young adults' ministry at our church). I gave massages the majority of the time. It was fun. While I was there, I noticed a couple of bags of clothes on the floor. I inquired about them and found out they were clothes that people brought that they didn't want or that didn't fit them anymore and they were up for grabs. I ended up taking a whole bag home! I got a lot of nice stuff, things I needed, and it was all for free! All of this makes me think of the verses of Scripture in Matthew 6:31-33 that talk about how we must not worry about how we are going to get our needs met, but instead seek first the Kingdom of God and His righteousness. He promises that if we do this all our needs will be provided for. It also says, in verse 31, that the Father knows what we need. I have learned that sometimes we *think* we need a certain thing but, in all reality, we just *want* it. I have also learned that God knows what is best for us, and if we don't get what we want, we still need to continue to trust the Lord, seek Him first, and not be bitter and try to get what we want in some other way. It's not worth it. Well, I'm still learning this. But I know it's true, I just need to keep reminding myself of it.

Questions:

1. How would you rate your overall level of passion for God from 1-10, 10 being very passionate? If your level is low, ask God why, and consider making more of an effort to surround yourself with people who are very passionate about God.

2. Do you feel a strong sense of connection to the body of Christ throughout the world? If not, consider praying for the Body of Christ around the world more.

3. Is there anything from your past that you feel like God wants you to go back and deal with? If yes, write about it and ask God what He wants you to hold on to or learn, and what He wants you to let go of. Write down your conversation with God. If you are really struggling with it, seek counseling from others believers and leaders in your life.

4. List some ways that God has provided for you in life.

5. Make a list of things you feel you need. Now ask God what He thinks about your list. Write down what He says.

Chapter 18

(April 8, 2004)

Lately, the Holy Spirit has been leading me back through old journal entries from when I first gave my heart to the Lord. This June it will have been three years since I surrendered my life to Christ. God has brought me *so* far. My cup overflows (Psalm 23:5)!

Thank You
by: Me

I reach out for You,
and You gently lift me up.
With loving arms You embrace me,
and hold me close to Your heart,
I cherish Your Words,
they make me strong,
They are to me
like a sweet, sweet song.
Thank You.

(April 19, 2004)

Lately, God has been allowing me to be in circumstances that have tested my character. One challenge I've been faced with, especially this past week, is people being angry with me. Some of the reasons were partially my fault and some reasons were not. It was weird, actually. People are very rarely upset with me, but then in one week, four people were upset with me. I have been pleased with my responses, thanks be to God. The Holy Spirit really helped me by reminding me of all kinds of Scriptures that specifically applied to the situations I was faced with, and by giving me the ability to discern (for the most part) what was from God and what was not—especially in my attitudes toward the people who were upset with me.

I realized that it is way too easy to get mad right back at someone who is mad at me, instead of taking the time to judge my own actions to see if I misbehaved in any way (Matthew 5:1-6). Even if I *didn't* do anything wrong, I know that I don't have the right to treat the person who wronged me poorly. Romans 12:21 says, "Do not be overcome by evil, but overcome evil with good." The world would say the complete opposite. It would say you overcome evil with more evil. This is not the way of God's Kingdom though. Jesus died for those who persecuted Him. While He was being nailed to the Cross, He even said, "Father, forgive them, for they do not know what they are doing" (Luke 23:34). How much more powerful is love verses hate?! Let us walk in the way of love (Ephesians 5:2).

Lord, thank you for showing me Your ways and helping me to apply them to my life. To You be all the glory, forever and ever, Amen.

(May 2, 2004)

It's been a while since I've written anything. First of all, God has been teaching me, in the midst of trying circumstances, how to be encouraged and excited instead of discouraged and depressed. There are two crisis situations going on in the lives of two families that are very close to me—my own family and my best friends family.

Recently, my brother got into some trouble with the law and got put in jail for a couple of days right away. Then he went to court last Monday and Tuesday. He was found guilty on three charges, and was taken to jail right away to wait out the time until his sentencing. I know it was definitely a shock to my family because things seemed to be looking up. Mom and Janet watched as he was taken away in handcuffs, which of course was very upsetting to them.

I knew Mike's court dates were at the end of April, but I wasn't sure of the exact days. I had a bad day on Tuesday, and I couldn't really pinpoint a clear reason why. When I got home later that night, it quickly became clear to me. I saw a note on the kitchen counter that said to "call home as soon as possible." I felt sick to my stomach. When I called home, I talked to my mom and she told me what had happened with Michael. I could tell she had been crying. During our conversation, she asked me if I would call Scott and tell him. Scott has a very tender heart for Michael, and my mom knows that. I told her that I would. She could hardly say goodbye. It broke my heart that I couldn't give her a big hug right then and there.

Now, calling Scott would mean breaking our agreement to not talk for the last three months of Master's Commission. I felt like it was okay to call him though. I could tell he was surprised to hear my voice. He asked me how I was doing, and I began telling him what had happened with my brother. He was very compassionate and, not to my surprise he already kind of had an idea of what was happening. He said that, not long ago, God gave him a vision about Michael, and that he's been praying a lot for him and my family and me. It was really nice talking to him. I am not sure what our future holds, but I sure do appreciate his friendship at this time in my life. He has really helped stir a desire in me to go deeper with God.

Another crisis close to my heart has been the marital conflict between an aunt and uncle of mine that I'm very close to. It's been serious for the past year or two. It just hurts so bad to see people you love go through difficult things.

(May 7, 2004)

I went to visit Michael last night. I didn't know what to expect. I knew he was really frustrated and angry about the whole situation, and I was really hoping to be a source of encouragement to him. It was so weird having to talk to him on a phone while looking at him through a pane of glass. It was a horrible feeling actually, being separated like that. I can only imagine how God must feel. As Michael and I were talking, I mentioned that he looked really clean. He replied that there wasn't much else to do there except clean yourself and comb your hair. God helped me to see that he wasn't only becoming more physically clean, but he was also becoming more spiritually clean.

He showed me that, as Michael is brushing the tangles and knots out of his hair, He is brushing the tangles and knots out of his soul. I know when God does some rearranging or purifying in our lives, it's usually not very pleasant, but God has helped me to see that it's okay to be frustrated and angry; it's part of the process, but it's just not okay to stay there. We need to come to a place where we realize some changes need to be made, then trust God that it's for the best. I am confident that my brother will be okay. I know he's right where God wants him. God has also shown me that it's important to continue to pray for him. I've learned that many times our answers are waiting for our prayers.

Questions:

1. How long has it been since you've surrendered your life to Christ? If you haven't yet, why not?

2. Write a letter or poem or song of thanks to God for His faithfulness in your life up to this point.

3. List a circumstance that you are in (or have recently been in) that has been a true test of your character. How have your actions measured up to the Word of God? What did you learn, specifically about yourself, through it all?

4. Are there currently any crisis situations happening in your life or the lives of people close to you? How are you handling them? If you are really struggling write a prayer asking God to help you trust Him and see how He is working in the situation. If you can't see Him working, pray for His intervention and let the peace of God guard your heart and mind (Philippians 4:6-7).

5. Is God currently doing any rearranging or purifying in your life? Describe the process and what you think God's purpose in all of it is. If you are not sure, just ask.

6. What is your understanding of prayer? Include Scripture references.

Chapter 19

(April 14, 2004)

So, we have about three weeks left of school. Lately I've been praying and asking God where I am spiritually, and if there is anything else that He still wants me to work on this year. I've realized, especially when our assistant director Kate addressed it to the whole group, that I haven't been giving my all. I've realized that I can coast through things and be okay, but how is that helping me? I've also realized that I am good at making excuses. I expressed all of this to the group. It is very humbling to be open and honest with others about things that I'm struggling with, especially my peers and leaders.

I feel like people put me up on a pedestal that I don't deserve to be on sometimes, but because it feels so good to be up there and have people respect and admire me like that, it's not so easy to step down. I know that I need to though. "Pride goes before destruction, a haughty spirit before a fall" (Proverbs 16:18). I know that God has been doing amazing things in and through me, but I feel like He wants me to deal with some new things. I'm slightly nervous, but I know it's going to be worth it.

(May 27, 2004)

God to me:

> I am so proud of you. Blessed are you, because I have put My Spirit in you, because I have granted you a willing spirit to sustain you. I have given you these things because you have asked for them. I desire to give you good gifts. I desire to surprise you and put joy in your heart. I love to see a smile on your face. It hurts Me to see you hurting. It makes My heart ache when your heart aches. I desire to set you free from things that are holding you back. I desire to make you strong. I desire that you would trust Me more. Trust Me that I will make your heart full. You don't need to go seeking on your own. I have already provided everything you need. **You just need to trust Me and be patient.** Because you are willing, I will do great things in and through you. Because you are willing, I will pour out so much blessing that even if you tried to contain it, you wouldn't be able to. I have built the set. I have set the stage. I have put everything in order. Now, let your light shine. You are a star.

Completion of Reality Masters Commission

(June 1, 2004)

I am so thankful for everyone here at Mansfield First Assembly of God. They've been like family to me this year. I hope that I never take for granted that there was always somebody to talk to, and if ever I was struggling, someone was always there to help me through it. I have learned so much this year. I've learned a lot about myself and a lot about God. I've learned the importance of team work; that team work is not always easy, especially when there are a lot of different personalities in the mix. I've learned that communication is definitely an important skill to obtain and excel in, especially if you are in any sort of leadership position. I've learned that another very important thing for leaders to do is to let their hearts be seen. People need to know your intentions and your heart. It's easy to get upset with people when you don't know their hearts and as I have mentioned earlier, the devil would love to cause as much division as possible, especially in the Church. I've also learned that you've not failed unless you've given up, and that God's grace is sufficient (2 Corinthians 12:9).

Tonight was a very defining moment for me. We all met at the church at 11 p.m. and had a time where we shared our favorite memories from this year. Then Andy and Kate gave each of us words of encouragement and advice. Both Andy and Kate said that they saw me as a very genuine and sincere person with a pure heart. Those were very encouraging things to hear, because I feel like people take me the wrong way sometimes, and I often battle with thoughts in my mind that tell me that I'm just doing things for my own personal gain. I know in my heart that I truly care about others, though, and I want to help where I can. I know I'm not perfect, and I have my selfish moments, but at my core I want to do the right thing. It was healing and encouraging to have them recognize this about me.

God to me:

> My child, you have asked so much of Me, and I have heard your prayers and I am faithful to fulfill My promises, **but you must be patient.** I know you've noticed the ability you now have to think positively through difficult situations. I've brought

that to your attention so you would know that I reward those who earnestly seek Me (Hebrews 11:6). You are so rich spiritually, and even though you can't see it all now, it doesn't change the fact that you are. I know your heart and I know you don't want to disappoint Me. I know you are thankful for everything I've done for you. Breathe! I know you want to be the best you can for Me. I promise I will keep you. I won't let you be satisfied with anything or anyone but Me. You have My word. I need you to help me out with something though. I need you to let Me heal you. You are still carrying a lot of emotional pain. I need you to trust Me and surrender those negative thoughts to Me. They will not add anything to your life. You need to recognize that those thoughts are from Satan, and he is trying to steal away the joy I've given you. Don't let him.

(June 14, 2004)

How are you so patient, Lord?

God to me:

Growing in patience is going to take time. You will need My help. Keep seeking Me. Remain in Me. Remember, you can do nothing apart from Me. When you step out in faith, it is not your strength, but Mine. It is not for you alone to carry such a heavy burden. You will fall if you try to live a life of faith without Me. Remain in Me. I am the vine and you are the branch (John 15:5).

God to me:

> I am bringing order into your life. This means I had to take some pieces from where they used to be, and I am putting them where they need to be. I know it feels like it's hard to get a grasp on things right now, but I will make the picture clear before you. Just keep doing what you are doing. Keep coming to Me for comfort and understanding. Keep reminding yourself of My faithfulness. Keep your eyes and heart fixed on Me. I will see you through. I will show you the way and it's going to be amazing!

(June 18, 2004)

You Are
by: Me

You sustain me, Oh Lord,
Your affections are for me.
You are ever with me,
I will rest in You.

You have put a song in my heart,
and made my steps light.
You have given me joy,
You are my delight.

Questions:

1. Pray and ask God to reveal one thing He wants you to work on right now. Write down your answer. If there is more than one thing, thats okay, just be careful to seek God about it and not to just start writing down everything you know you need to work on. If you try to tackle too much at once you might

get overwhelmed and quit all together. *Trust me, I know.* Let the Holy Spirit lead you. Keep a record of your progress.

2. Write down the definition of "pride." Now be honest about when you struggle with it.

3. Ask God what His desires are for you and write them down. Include some Scripture references. Note that everything that God desires for you is born out of a heart of unconditional love for you. Filter your answer through this.

4. Oftentimes when God speaks to us, He is counteracting fears or lies we are believing. Look back through what you just wrote and see if you can pick out any fears or lies God was trying to counteract in you.

5. List five (or more!) of the most important lessons you've learned in life so far.

6. Describe a defining moment in your life.

7. List some of your character qualities that have improved since you became a Christian.

8. Are you carrying any emotional pain that you haven't allowed God to deal with? If your answer is yes, close your eyes and think specifically about the moment it entered into your life. Ask the Holy Spirit to guide you. After the scene is clear in your mind, find Jesus there (because He was there), and

write down what He is doing and saying in the memory. Talk about your answer with a trusted, mature believer or Christian leader to make sure what you are believing is from God.

9. Write a letter of thanks to God.

Chapter 20

(June 22, 2004)

What I am about to write is a *huge* answer to prayer! So here goes… I went to visit Michael again at the end of May. I didn't know what to expect. The last time I visited him, he seemed very frustrated and angry. To my delight, this time was a *very* different experience. I noticed right away that there was something different about him, evidenced by the smile on his face when he came out. When I picked up the phone, I asked him how he was doing and he said, "Well as good as I can be." It was clear to me by his response and the smile on his face that something had changed in him for the better. I soon found out the source of this change.

He went on to tell me that he had made two good Christians friends in there, and that he also met someone from Israel who was teaching him some Hebrew! He said it was "Wild!" He also told me that he had been praying and reading his Bible a lot, and with an almost surprised expression he said, "And I've been liking it!" He even quoted a couple of his favorite Scripture verses to me along with the references. It quickly became clear to me that the same Spirit that I received when I first gave my heart to the Lord was now living in him! I thought this was the case, but I wasn't sure.

One night previous to this visit, between the time that Michael first went to jail and his court date, I was home visiting and I noticed him heading outside. I asked him where he was going and he said that he was going to see a friend. I then asked if I could tag along. He said, "Yeah, sure." When I sat down in the passenger seat of his car and shut the door, he immediately looked over at me and said in a proud, excited tone, "Guess what?... I found God." I was surprised and delighted to hear him say this, and I inquired as to how. He said that when he first went to jail, he felt so scared and alone that first night. As he was sitting there in that cold, dark jail cell all alone, he cried out to God for help. He went on to say that he immediately felt Jesus there with him, with a very strong sense that He was holding his hand, and he just knew he needed to get his life right.

A week or two after I visited Michael, I talked to him on the phone and I was happy to learn that he was still doing really well. He told me that he had been reading his Bible more and was surprised at the things he's been reading, especially some of the Scriptures that directly apply to his exact situation. I told him (and he agreed with me) that even though the Bible was written a long time ago, it is still very relevant to our lives today. He went on to tell me that he thinks the reason he got sent back to jail was because God didn't think he was ready to get out yet; because he wasn't fixing things he knew he needed to. I was encouraged by the understanding he has about his situation and about life in general. He said that he believes whatever happens is supposed to happen because he's put it in God's hands.

I know that the Spirit of God is the only one who can give someone that kind of understanding and peace. Michael went on to say that there was one night that he just broke down and started crying, not because he was sad, but because he was so happy. I am very familiar with that feeling. It comes when you put your faith in Jesus and you have a deep confidence and peace that He is with you and you will be okay. Then I said to him, "Now you know why I do what I do," and he said, "Yeah, totally." He then went on to tell me that he knew he needed to change things in his life.

I suggested getting plugged into a church somewhere and going to Bible studies. He liked the idea.

Michael's sentencing was June 15th. Everyone from our family came, as well as Aunt Pat and Uncle Paul, and Michael's friend Johnny. It was supposed to be at 10 a.m., but was delayed until 3 p.m. It was obvious that everyone's stomachs were in knots. I was sitting beside Liz and she held my hand firmly the entire time. The sentencing was hard. It was like a hammer hitting all of our hearts as the prosecutor and the judge recalled all of Michael's offenses from the time he was fifteen years old up until now. It was hard to keep hate from rising up against the people who were trying to get someone we loved so dearly thrown into prison. I think everyone agreed at the end of the day that there were consequences that needed to be paid for his actions, but not everyone agreed on the method of payment.

Michael was sentenced to three years in prison, with the possibility of getting out after six months on good behavior. The sentence was worse than we expected. Michael was very mature about it though. I was very proud of him. When they let him come back to us to tell us goodbye, I gave him a hug and told him he did a good job. He didn't say anything back to me. He kept a straight face pretty much the whole time. He couldn't hug us back because he had handcuffs on. Dad shook his hand. It was a heart wrenching moment. Nobody cried during the trial, but after Michael left, the tears were flowing.

Questions:

1. Recount a big answer to prayer. It can be about you or someone close to you.

2. Do you believe that the Bible is still relevant today? If yes, why? Include a few Scripture references. If no, then why not?

3. Describe a moment where you felt a deep confidence and peace that God was in control and that you would be okay.

Chapter 21

(July 23, 2004)

As I was reading through my Bible this morning, I stopped for a moment and realized that I hadn't had an amazing moment with God lately. Instead of being sad, I thanked the Lord that He would show Himself strong in my life again. At that very moment, I saw a very clear vision in my mind of Jesus placing His hand on me and asking God to open my eyes so that I might see Him more clearly; I knew Jesus was asking this of the Father for me because of my faith. After the Lord prayed for me, I was reminded of a dream I had last night. I dreamt I was getting my eyes checked and the doctor said that I had some dust in my eyes. His prescription was to have someone take a small tool that blew air out of the end and blow the dust out of my eyes. It didn't hurt. I just remember my eyes watering a lot.

Oh Lord, thank You for caring for me so much. Oh that my eyes would be opened more and more so that I could gaze more fully upon Your beauty.

(July 24, 2004)

God to me:

> Don't talk defeat. Talk victory. People need to hear your testimony.
> You need to hear your testimony! Your victory is in your praise. Remember My faithfulness and where I brought you from. Watch your words. Speak faith.

Questions:

1. Describe your last amazing moment with God. If you've never had an amazing moment with God, stop and ask God to reveal His love for you. It might be helpful to close your eyes and imagine yourself somewhere with God, just you and Him. Wait for Him. Write down your experience and anything He says to you.

2. Write down your testimony, the moment you became born again (John 1:12; Romans 10:9; 2 Corinthians 5:27; Galatians 3:26; 1 Peter 1:23). You can put as much or as little detail in it as you want.

3. Think of a situation in your life that you are struggling with. Write it down. Now write a proclamation of victory over the situation. In other words, proclaim God's promises over it. Include some Scripture references.

Chapter 22

(July 27, 2004)

So, I've been starting to question (only a little at first, but it's getting stronger) whether or not I should attend a second year of Reality Master's Commission. I had a dream last night about being in a beautiful house, and I was wondering around it and I got lost. The owner of the house found me, directed me outside, and pointed me in the direction of a school. When I got outside, I turned around and noticed that the house (which was more like a mansion) was connected to a very old castle. It was all made of stone and it looked like it was built into the side of a mountain. I remember telling someone that the new house was built over the old one. I could tell this because some of the old castle stone looked like it had been replaced with new stone. I pointed out how beautiful it was.

God showed me that the mansion in my dream represented me, half new and half old and crumbling. The new represented Jesus' sanctifying work that has been accomplished in my life so far, and the old represented the work that still needs to be done.

I've told people the reason that I was planning on going back for a second year of Master's Commission was because I felt like God wasn't finished with me there yet. The fact that I had the intention of going to school in my dream makes me think that I am still supposed to go back. Yet in my dream, instead of heading straight for school, I stopped and talked to people who were standing on the grass outside. I think I remember there being a fence around the school. It seemed so far in the distance but the people were right in front of me. I'm not sure what this means.

Lord, I give these thoughts and questions to You. Test them and weigh them. Lead me down Your path for my life. Thank You for the answer that You're going to give me. Thank You that You are going to make everything come together and make perfect sense. Thank You that You are going to work things out so that You will be glorified. This is what I want Lord, for You to be glorified in and through me, forever and ever. Amen.

*(*August 17, 2004)

Okay… so a lot has changed since the last time I wrote. The last thing I wrote about was not knowing whether or not I was supposed to attend a second year of Reality Master's Commission. Well, I decided not to make a final decision until I got back from volunteering with *Relevant Magazine* at Kingdom Bound Christian Music Festival in New York (*Relevant Magazine* is a progressive Christian magazine geared for young adults). How did that all come about? Well, I'm glad you asked. I will explain in a minute. The second thing that has changed is my relationship with Scott. God has recently made it very clear that Scott and I are not meant to be together. It was difficult for both of us to accept this at first, because there were several times throughout our relationship that we felt very strongly that our closeness was pointing toward a future. Yet, it wasn't long after I received a certain email from Pastor David's wife Kathy that I had peace in my heart that ending our relationship was the right thing to do.

So here's the story. One day toward the end of May, Kathy sent me an email saying that God had made it very clear to her, her husband David, and another woman at the church that Scott and I weren't meant to be married. She explained to me in the email that she was very hesitant to share this with me, because she didn't want to be like one of those meddling Christians. But, after David asked God directly if Scott and I were meant to be married and he heard God very clearly say, "No," and another woman from the church had a very vivid dream that if Scott and I got married it would end in disaster, she decided that she had better email me and tell me what God had revealed to them. I was very thankful for her faithfulness in being obedient to God in this matter because, even though there were moments where I felt very sure that Scott and I were meant to be together, there were also moments when I wasn't so sure. Even though it was difficult to let Scott go, I knew in my heart that it was the right thing to do.

Scott is a great guy and I am thankful for the time our paths crossed. Now that we have gone our separate ways, though, this experience has caused me to be very curious about who God has set apart for me. Time will tell I guess... *until then, please help me to be patient and wait on You, Lord.*

So, now to explain how I ended up volunteering with *Relevant Magazine* at Kingdom Bound Christian Music Festival in New York. Well, while attending Corner Stone Christian Music Festival in Illinois not long ago with my good friend Penny from Reality Master's Commission, I formed a relationship with a guy named Kenny who was working at the *Relevant Magazine* booth. He talked me into getting a magazine subscription, which didn't take much effort, because I *really* like the magazine. We ended up talking for a little bit afterwards, just simple basic stuff—like where you're from, what you do, etc. Before I left, he said I should come back later and maybe give him my email address or something. That kind of caught me off guard. I didn't expect it. I mean...I hoped for it because he was really cute!

I ended up going back at the end of the night with the intention of giving him my email address, but when I got there, another girl, who happened to be *really* pretty, was helping out. I didn't know what her relationship with him was, and I didn't feel like getting any dirty looks (plus I was a little nervous), so I just walked away. After a few minutes of trying to muster up some courage, I returned to the table (the really pretty girl was still there), and I chickened out again! After failing at my mission twice, I went outside and stood on the opposite side of the path outside the back of the tent where Kenny was. I didn't know what to do. I felt very torn. Finally I prayed, "Lord, please give me some sort of sign to let me know whether or not I should go talk to him." Shortly after I prayed that prayer, Kenny came out of the back of the tent onto the path where I was! It startled me. I pretended like I was just walking by, and acted surprised to see him. We talked for a little bit and I gave him my email address. Mission complete!

So, Kenny ended up emailing me about a week after the event. I emailed him back and told him a little bit more about myself, including my testimony. He wrote back, not really responding to what I wrote, but asking me if I would be interested in helping out at the Relevant booth at Kingdom Bound Music Festival in New York. He said that I wouldn't have to worry about getting a ticket or a place to stay or food to eat, they would provide it all! All I had to do was show up and work the booth. Well, let me tell you, I was super excited! As soon as I finished reading the email, I told Butch and Joyce (with whom I was still living), then I called my work to see if I could get those days off.

Butch and Joyce were really happy for me *and* I was able to get the days off work! The festival was August 1 through 4. I decided that I would make this a time where I would really seek God about whether or not I was supposed to go back to Reality Master's Commission for a second year. I went by myself, and it was really nice. I've really been enjoying my alone time lately. The drive wasn't too bad, only five and a half hours. The guys made me feel very welcome and comfortable right away when I got there. There was another guy that came along to help from Michigan named Matt. He is a lot of fun and really nice too.

I had such a great time! I met a lot of nice people. I worked the booth most of the time. I did take a few breaks here and there, during which I went to listen to some bands and hear some teaching. Adrian, the marketing manager for the magazine, definitely appreciated our help. They had two booths set up, and it was only him and two other guys, Kenny and Tyler. God set up a lot of really cool divine appointments with people that came to the booth inquiring about the magazine. I felt extra sensitive to the Holy Spirit, and I was able to share my testimony and different things I've learned on my Christian journey thus far with several people. I loved it!

Anyway, I decided during this time that I wasn't going to return to Reality Master's Commission for a second year. I didn't get any real direct signs from God. It kind of felt more like God was leaving it up to me. It's not that I don't totally believe in the school. I think Master's Commission is amazing and I would highly recommend it to any young adult who is really serious about God and wants to grow in their faith and be equipped for ministry. I am very thankful for my time as a student at Reality Master's Commission. I really do feel like God is leading me in a different direction now, though. On that note, I am planning on moving to Orlando, Florida! Why Orlando, you ask? Well, that's a great question. One that I've had to answer quite a few times in the past few days.

So here goes. After I returned from Kingdom Bound, before I knew that Orlando was my next step, God confirmed that He wanted to move me from where I was through a vision I had one day while I was praying. In my vision I saw myself floating in the sky. I knew it was God who had lifted me up from where I was and was moving me to a new place, but I didn't know where it was because there was a cloud surrounding me. Thankfully, it wasn't long before God lifted the cloud and made my next step clear.

One day, while driving to work, I was praying yet again about where I was supposed to go next. In my mind I heard God clearly say, "You've asked Me where I want you to go. Now I'm asking you, where do *you* want to go?" I said, "Well, if it's up to me Lord, I want to go to Orlando." Ever since I learned that Relevant Media Company is based out of Orlando, I wanted to move there. Their mission statement is so similar to my personal one it's almost scary, and I would love to get involved with them in one way or another. Orlando also seems like an exciting place to live. I didn't want to move there just because *I* wanted to though. I wanted to move there because I knew that it was something God wanted me to do.

After I told the Lord that I wanted to move to Orlando, I clearly heard Him say, "Well then, stop praying about where you are supposed to go, and start praying about what you're supposed to do when you get there." When I heard this, I felt the confusion about my next step lift off of me. It was immediately replaced with a strong sense of confidence that Orlando was where God was leading me next, and a bubbling sense of excitement to move there. This makes me think of Psalm 37:4 which says, "Take delight in the Lord, and he will give you the desires of your heart."

It was relieving to finally have a clear sense of direction. Now all I needed to do was figure out how and when. After about a week or so of not having any clear direction in regard to when I was supposed to move to Orlando and how I was going to get there, I began to question if I was really supposed to move there. As I began to ask this question, I felt the cloud of confusion that had just recently lifted off of me return. I shouldn't have been surprised. I had asked the Lord for wisdom, and at one point I was confident that He gave me an answer; and now, just because a week had passed and I couldn't work out some details, I began to doubt. I have been praying and asking God to help me walk by faith and not by sight. I am learning that this means boldly stepping out in the direction I feel God is leading me in and trusting that He will take care of the details.

Shortly afterward, in the midst of my discouragement and confusion, Joyce sat me down and talked to me in the manner I suppose she would talk to one of her own children. She said that I couldn't just sit around and wait for something to happen, which had sort of been the nature of my actions for the past week. She went on to tell me that she and Butch had been talking. They had decided that, because I had decided not to return to Reality Master's Commission for a second year, they felt that they needed to give me a timeframe to move out by. She was really kind and gentle about it. My reaction was that of thankfulness. I took it as a confirmation that I was in fact supposed to move to Orlando, like God was giving me a little shove in that direction.

A renewed sense of faith rose up in me and I made a definite decision that day that I would move to Orlando. In that very same day, I packed up all my stuff and moved back in with my parents. Joyce didn't want me to feel like I needed to move out that same day, but I didn't see a good reason to stay there any longer. Plus, I thought it would be easier for me to figure out details for my move at my parents, and I wanted to be able to spend some good quality time with them before I made this big move anyway.

I've already covered all my bases. I talked to my work about my decision to move to Orlando, and the owner was very understanding. She was sad to see me go, but excited for me. I've talked to Andy and Kate about my decision to not return to Reality Master's Commission for a second year. They were sad, but at the same time they were very supportive and encouraging. They seemed to have no doubt I made my decision based on what I believed God was leading me to do, which was very encouraging to me. My parents and Butch and Joyce have made sure that I know that I'm going to have to work very hard. They also stressed the fact that this move will mean that I will have to handle a lot more responsibility. I've reassured them that I'm aware of this and that I feel up to the task. I've been amazed at how understanding and supportive everyone has been. Just another confirmation to me that I'm on the right track.

So, my initial plan was, after staying at my parents for a little over a month, to move in with some of my dad's good friends in Orlando until I could afford a place of my own. I forgot they even lived there! These plans quickly changed though. Read on.

A few weeks after I had moved back in with my parents, Adrian, the marketing manager of *Relevant Magazine*, said that I could work the Relevant booth at another Christian music festival in Pennsylvania called "Purple Door." Yay! I learned while I was there that Purple Door was Relevant's last festival for the summer, and that after it was over, Adrian and the intern were heading back to Orlando. After Adrian told me this, I mentioned to him that I was planning on moving to Orlando in the near future. He then invited me to Orlando to check it out to see if I liked it before I packed up everything and moved down there. I agreed that this was an excellent idea, and thanked him for the invite. Matthew, the guy from Michigan that came to help out at Kingdom bound, wanted to visited Orlando too. We decided to drive down together. It was a long, fun drive that we ended up stretching out over two days. We stayed the night at his aunt's house. She was super nice.

While in Orlando, Adrian gave us a tour of Relevant Media Company and introduced us to some of the other employees and interns! They were all so nice. It was an extremely exciting and inspiring experience. We also went to a young adults' service on Thursday night at a church called "Church in the Son" where Adrian attends when he can. I loved it! After the service, some people from the church came up and talked to me, one of them being a girl named Natalie. Natalie asked me some questions about myself, and I ended up telling her that I was planning on moving to Orlando in the near future. She asked me if I had a place to stay yet, and informed me that a girl in her small group named Meredith was looking for another roommate! I told her that I would love to talk to Meredith about it, and she gave me

Meredith's number. When I prayed about it later, I saw a very clear vision of two hands. When I asked God what this meant, He revealed to me that the two hands represented a church family for me to be a part of and a good place to live. What joy was mine! When I called Meredith and explained my situation to her, she said I should totally come live with her, and that she couldn't wait to meet me! I wasn't surprised by her response, and of course I accepted her offer!

Thank You Lord for being so faithful to lead and guide me, and for making sure that I don't miss You. I am so excited to go on this journey with You.

Questions:

1. What is your personal mission statement? If you don't know what it is, I would highly recommend reading a book called *Chazown* by Craig Groeschel, the Senior Pastor of LifeChurch. TV. You can also visit their website at www.chazown.com and complete *The Chazown Experience* online for free!

2. What did you learn about God from this chapter?

Chapter 23

(August 31, 2004)

So, in a little over two weeks, I will be twenty-two years old! Wow, that's crazy to think about, but I like it! Anyways, I currently have a major change staring me in the face. Like I wrote earlier, I will be moving to Orlando, FL. I am planning on leaving in one month. I am excited, and also slightly nervous. My first priority when I get down there is to find a job. My second priority is to figure out if I can get involved with Relevant Media Company somehow. Deep down, I have a feeling that there is a bigger reason for me moving to Orlando which I'm not aware of yet. This makes me even more excited to go!

Like I said, I'm *really* excited, and slightly nervous. I'm excited because I know God is in it, but I'm slightly nervous because there's so much uncertainty, it's such a big move, and I will be really far away from my family. I feel like I've been in class for a while, learning what God wants me to do, and now the tests are starting to be handed out. Now, I like taking tests granted I know my stuff. I guess there's only one way to find out.

I know it's normal to feel nervous in a situation like this. I also know that God will help me. This gives me peace. I know I just need to stay focused on Him. I know that God is calling me out of my comfort zone so that I can learn how to trust Him more.

I feel like moving to Orlando is my first real adventure, my first real excursion into unknown territory. Kind of like a final exam to see if I'm ready to move on to the next grade level. My heart's desire in all of this is to stay strong in my relationship with the Lord and stay focused on what He's called me to do.

Help me, Lord!

(September 2, 2004)

Right now, my parents and I are currently on our way back from helping my older sister Liz move into her new apartment on the outskirts of Boston, MA, not far from where she'll be attending two years of graduate school at the Longy School of Music. She's been chosen to be among a small number of students that are accepted there each year. I called her soon after my parents and I left because, as I was turning to leave, I saw her face turn from an expression that communicated, "Everything is going to be okay," to, "Help! I'm here in this big place all alone!" I know it's definitely going to be challenging. If I were in her position, I would be feeling scared too. Well, I actually will be in her position very shortly, and that's *exactly* how I'm feeling! I've found that it's way easier to believe in someone else rather than yourself, mainly because we tend to focus on all our weaknesses and let those overshadow our strengths. Yet, as hard as it is to believe in yourself sometimes, I do know that when other people believe in you, it helps a lot.

On this same note: something very important that I've learned since I decided to move to Orlando is that *it's okay to be afraid, just don't let that fear hold you back.* One of my biggest fears during the process of preparing to move to Orlando has been that I didn't really hear from God to move there. Sometimes I've also caught myself being afraid that I won't be strong enough to be successful there. I don't like failing. Who does? I'm learning that sometimes (well most of the time) faith requires risk. If I want to grow in my faith, I have to be okay with failing sometimes, and just trust that God will cover me and help me get back up. Anyway, God has graciously calmed my fears again by confirming again that I did in fact hear from Him. One big way He did this was through the book I'm currently reading called *God Whispers* by Margaret Feinburg. The particular passage I'm referring to says:

> Hearing from God is worthless if you don't obey. Some people become so focused on discerning whether or not what they heard was from God that they never take the first step of obedience. They feel that if they don't have one hundred percent certainty, then everything will turn into a disaster. The fear of being wrong prevents them from ever having the opportunity to be right… God is a big God. He can handle it. He knows you are going to stumble and make mistakes. Remember, God looks at the heart. When He sees people stepping out—even if they are heading in the wrong direction—He can lovingly correct or even turn things around to use it for His glory. Think about it. Would you rather stand before God and say, "I wasn't sure it was you, so I didn't do anything," or, "I wasn't sure that it was you, so I stepped out in faith trusting you would correct me if I was wrong"?[7]

Those last words really hit me and gave me a newfound peace and excitement about moving to Orlando. After reading these passages, I was amazed at how much they directly applied to me and my current situation. I was really encouraged because I had already stepped out in faith and started moving in the direction that I believed God was leading me in, instead of letting my fears hold me back—thanks be to God!

I've learned that the process of hearing God's voice is one that should be done very carefully and with the help of the Bible and other solid Christians—especially when it comes to making major life decisions. God's voice isn't the only voice that is trying to get our attention. We need to be aware that the devil, the world, and our own fallen natures will be trying to have a say in our decision making process. When we are pretty sure that we're on the right track, though, and we've gotten counsel, then we need to step out in faith and trust that God will do His part.

Even though hearing God's voice can be hard, I believe with all my heart that every born again believer *can* know it, and *needs* to know it. God's voice is a vital, powerful weapon against the enemy, and a powerful tool to help build God's kingdom. John 10:27 says, "My sheep hear My voice; I know them, and they follow Me." I have learned that the more I surrender to Jesus' lordship in my life, the more I am obedient to follow Him no matter the cost, *the more time I spend being one of His "sheep,"* the easier it is for me to discern His voice. This has proved very true in my life so many times, and in the lives of many, many others.

Here are some things that I've done that have helped me become more able to discern God's voice:

1. Intentionally spend focused time with Him, reading and meditating on the Word.
2. Journal.
3. Praise and worship Him.
4. Remember His faithfulness in my life.
5. Talk with other Christians about what it means to be a Christian.
6. Study the Bible and other Christian books together with other believers.
7. Read books specifically about how to hear God's voice.

8. Try not to listen to or watch things that I know are blatantly evil.

There are a lot of good resources out there about how to hear God's voice. Just be sure that what you choose is Biblically sound.[8]

God can speak in many ways. Here are some of the main ways He speaks to us: the Bible, circumstances, people, thoughts in our minds, and strong impressions in our emotions. This last one can be especially tricky to discern. It's very helpful to test your motives to know whether a strong emotion you are feeling is from God or not. You can discern this by asking yourself why you want to do that thing. This is a really good question to ask, and it makes it a lot easier to see if what you heard or what you are feeling lines up with Biblical principles. Everything needs to be measured against the Bible (2 Timothy 3:16-17). If what you heard or are feeling led to do is something that wouldn't line up with Biblical principles, then it is *not* from God. I have found reading Philippians 2:3-8 to be especially helpful in the process of testing my motives. If you are struggling with principles in the Bible, pray and do your research. If you are still struggling, and even if you're not, it's good to talk to someone who is well studied in the Bible and can help bring some clarity and understanding. If you are questioning whether the Bible is the authoritative word of God, then you need to figure out where you stand on this before you can move on. Otherwise, you'll remain in a state of confusion and frustration. I can tell you that there are a lot of resources out there proving the legitimacy of the Holy Bible. I'm very confident that it can be trusted.[9]

Speaking of hearing God's voice….there is something else that just came to my mind that I recognize as a specific word from God for me. When my parents and older sister and I were sitting down eating some lunch at a Denny's in Boston, I brought up the fact that the intern application at *Relevant Magazine* said that you have to be in college. Obviously, I am not. When I brought this up, my mom said, "Well, obviously they see something in you they like." That made me feel better. Then I told them that one of the questions on the application asked where I saw myself in five years. I had no idea what to put. I mean, I have a lot of ideas, but I don't feel like I have a single set direction yet, so it's really hard to say where I'll be in five years. After quietly listening, my mom said something that really encouraged me—something that I believe was a divinely inspired word from God for me. She said, "Well, you can just tell them that in five years you will still be spreading the love of God." I'm not sure that will be enough for *Relevant Magazine*, which is okay, but it was sure enough to put my mind at ease about the future. *Thanks Mom!*

Questions:

1. Are you in a place where you really have to trust God?

2. What are some of your strengths? What are some of your weaknesses?

3. Look up Philippians 4:13, write it down, and make it a point to memorize this Scripture.

4. When do you feel closest to Jesus? For example, times of worship, journaling, etc.?

5. What would you say is the main way that God speaks to you?

6. Do you believe that the Holy Bible is the infallible, authoritative Word of God? If yes, why? Include Scripture references. If not, why not?

Chapter 24

(September 22, 2004)

The most amazing thing happened to me tonight! Well, first of all, I'm in Brentwood, TN. Brentwood is about ten minutes outside of Nashville. It also happens to be where Kenny is from (I had a crush on him for a little bit, but I've realized that he's not my type. Moving on). This is my first stop on my way down to Orlando, FL. Kenny graciously arranged for me to stay with his aunt and uncle here for a few nights. They are very generous and kind. After this, I will be staying with my best friend Cathy in Troy, AL, where she is attending Troy State University.

Anyway, I went to a concert tonight with Kenny and some of his friends. It was a lot of fun. Afterward, we went to a local gathering place for young adults. I met a really nice guy there named Timothy. At first, our conversation consisted of the usual questions you ask someone when you first meet them like, "What's your name? Where are you from? What do you do?" and the corresponding answers. He's from Australia! When I learned what he does for a living, he really had my attention, and God showed up in a *big* way.

He counsels prison inmates! As soon as I found this out, I began to tell him about my brother who is currently in prison, and how distressed my family and I are about it. Then, I talked to him about some other struggles my family members are going through, and how I hate it for them. From then on in our conversation, almost every word Timothy spoke to me literally felt like God speaking directly to me. At times, I felt God's presence so strong that I could hardly stand (he's a Christian by the way—he didn't say it right away, but it came up in conversation after we'd been talking for a bit).

God spoke some things through Timothy that really touched my heart and brought some much needed healing. He told me that my family would be okay, and that I'm doing all I can do to help, and that nothing they are going through is my fault. For some reason, when he said that "nothing they are going through was my fault," it was incredibly healing. I don't know why, but for some reason I'm carrying a lot of guilt about this. I guess I feel like I don't do enough to help.

He went on to say that I stuck out to him as being attractive (it surprised me to hear him say this, as I wasn't feeling very attractive *at all* tonight). When he said this, it reminded me of all the times that God has told me how beautiful He thinks I am, and that I should never settle for believing anything less about myself. Then he kept saying, "Don't ever settle!" After repeating "don't ever settle" several times, he said, "God has big plans for you. Dream *big*."

I was letting a few tears escape before this, but at this point, I broke. I desperately want to make a *big* difference for God. This is the most precious desire of my heart. Often times I feel so inadequate and sometimes this dream just feels so far out of reach, and I get really discouraged. I was feeling discouraged today about this very thing.... and here was this guy I had never met before telling me that God has *big* plans for me, to never settle, and to dream big. It was a very surreal moment. God is *so* good!

When Timothy spoke to me, he kept telling me to look at him. I know he said this because my head was bowed down the majority of the time. When I would look up at him with my tear-filled eyes, he would say, "I'm telling you the truth. I'm not a liar." This is yet another thing God has spoken to me over and over, mainly by way of telling me to trust Him. Timothy also kept telling me that everything would be okay. I told him that I knew it would, and that's why I was crying. My tears were tears of joy. I told him that I wished he knew how much of a miracle he was to me. He kept saying that he wished I would stop crying, because it was breaking his heart. Every time he said this it made me cry even more, because it made me think about all the times God has told me how He hates to see me hurting, and that it breaks His heart when my heart is broken. God knew just what I needed to hear, right when I needed to hear it. He was yet again overwhelming me with His awesome love, and giving me courage to live big for Him.

(October 5, 2004)

I made it! My drive down to Florida was great! I felt God's grace and peace with me really strong almost the entire time (obviously in Tennessee). I also had a really good time in Alabama with Cathy. I ended up staying there longer than I had originally planned due to "Jeanne," the most recent hurricane that came through. It knocked out the power at my new place, so instead of leaving from Cathy's on September 28 like I planned, I left October 4. I'm glad I got to stay a little longer. The day I got there, Cathy had just found out that she wouldn't be able to get into the nursing program there, and therefore had to transfer to another school. On top of that, the situation with her parents had gotten worse. As Cathy's "bestest friend in the whole wide world," I was really glad I could be there for her during this extremely difficult time in her life. This was a total gift from God for both of us.

On a lighter note, my new roommates are awesome! Meredith and I get along really great. Her parents own the townhouse that we're living in, and we just pay them rent. My other roommate's name is Kelly. I haven't really talked to her much, but she seems nice. We all went to the young adults' service tonight at Church in the Son—the "Living Room." I'm really excited about being a part of this church. I've already met so many nice people.

I am so excited to be on this journey with You, Lord. Thank You for guiding my steps and providing for me, just like You said You would. You are so faithful and trustworthy. Please help me to continue to trust in You for all of my needs.

Questions:

1. Recount a moment (or a few moments) in your life where God has shown up in a powerful way, and write down what He communicated to you in those moments.

2. What is your biggest dream?

3. What would you say or do for a friend who is going through a hard time? Note: It is helpful to put yourself in their shoes. For example, treat them how you would want to be treated. Also equally important, if not more—ask for the Holy Spirit's guidance.

4. Are you a part of a church family? Are you excited about being a part of it?

Chapter 25

(October 16, 2004)

Okay, so I had an emotional break down yesterday. It was after I went to a job interview that I was really excited about and had really high hopes for. I was told that the lady I needed to meet with wouldn't be able to meet with me until Tuesday. Well, yesterday was Friday, which means that I need to wait three more days! On Monday, I will have been in Orlando for two weeks. I was hoping to have some sort of job secured by now, so needless to say, I was feeling really discouraged after being told that I needed to wait longer to have that security in place. Yesterday I gave into the temptation to emotionally beat myself up and fall into doubt. I was thinking things like, "I'm lazy. I'm not working hard enough to get a job. I'm not strong enough." I also went back to wrestling with the question of whether moving to Orlando was God's desire, or if I was just making it all up in my head. The Holy Spirit helped me to see my negativity and questioning for what is was—me believing lies and not trusting God.

Then the Holy Spirit reminded me of what God had spoken to me a couple of days ago, about how doubt was trying to creep its way into my heart and mind, and that I mustn't let it. I knew that if I continued to falter on this subject, I would crumble like this every time a trial came my way, which I know is sure to happen more. It seems so silly to me now as I'm writing this, that I let myself fall into doubt again. How many times has God clearly confirmed that He was the one leading me down here and that He will never leave me or forsake me? How many times does He have to confirm it?

God didn't make me feel bad about my moment of weakness. He told me that my faith is being tested and strengthened (I am reminded of the multiple times that I have heard the phrase "faith that is not tested is no faith at all"). He also reminded me that I can't live a life of faith in my own strength; I need to remain in Him (John 15:5).

Yesterday, I learned that I normally suppress a lot of my negative emotions in an attempt to stay positive. I guess I feel like if I express any kind of negative emotions, like fear or doubt, then I'm letting the devil win. I've learned that keeping negative emotions bottled up like this isn't healthy, because it's not a matter of *if* negative emotions will rise to the surface, but *when,* and it's really hard to handle a lot of negative emotions all at once (hence my emotional breakdown yesterday). Luckily, God helped me snap out of it before I did anything rash, like pack up all my stuff and go home. It's clear to me as I think about the Psalms of David (specifically the ones where he was really struggling), that God wants us to express how we are feeling to Him—not just the positive, but the negative as well. The only time we are letting the devil win is if we hold onto our negative emotions and let them eat away at our faith. We need to learn what *God* has to say and hold on to that.

I know that another reason I'm struggling is because I'm bored. In Master's Commission, I was always busy doing exciting things for God. Now, not so much. At least that's what it feels like. I'm also feeling really lonely. I consciously made this choice to step out in faith, though. Did I think it was going to be easy?

In other news, I went to a women's meeting at church last night called "Extreme Makeover." The pastor's wife talked about how many of the things women deal with (like rejection, depression, and low self-esteem) are all a result of believing lies from the enemy about themselves. I know that this is true, but for some reason I still deal with these things on occasion, especially yesterday morning. I wanted someone to pray for me last night, but I felt like I would just hear the same things I've already heard, and I didn't see how that was going to help me if it hasn't helped me already. Normally, I wouldn't listen to that kind of thought. I guess I was just feeling fed up last night. I was sick of getting prayer for things I feel like I should be over by now. Normally, when someone prays for me I tend to feel better, but only for a short while. Then it will come back… and I'm sick of it!! I'm done with feelings! I want something that is going to last. I am to the point now where I would rather feel crappy than believe that everything is okay when it really isn't.

So what's it gonna take, and where does God and faith come into all of this? Right now my spirit is screaming inside of me that God is very much in all of this, that He is weeding out the bad stuff to make room for the good, that He is putting everything I believe to the test and separating the lies from the truth, and that I *am* in fact moving forward in Him.

I've learned that it's not pretty when God shines His light on sin in our lives. Every time God has shined His light on sin in my life, I can't help but cringe that something so ugly has been living inside of me. It's so incredibly liberating to know that my sin does not define who I am. Through faith in Jesus, I am washed white as snow, and any sin I am struggling with no longer has the power to condemn me (Isaiah 1:18; Psalm 51:7). It does, however, have the power to steal away the joy, peace, and freedom that God desires me to have in this life. That's why it's so important that I continue to let God into the deep recesses of my soul, accept His unconditional love for me, and stand on His truth in even greater ways. *That's what it's gonna take!* Then I will have the strength to say no to sin, and it will no longer have any power over me. I might feel like I'm dying at the time, but I know that the only thing that will die will be my sinful nature, and I say, "Goodbye to bad rubbish!" The most encouraging thing to me through all of this is that I've never doubted God's love for me. I've always known that He would never give up on me. I know I have accepted this truth and it has been my anchor. Now, I just need to trust Him with all of the other details of my life, namely my hopes and dreams.

I'm thankful that God is allowing me to go through this, because I know that I will come out better on the other end. It's what I've been praying for. I want to get to a place where there is nothing inside of me that will hold God back from working through me in powerful ways.

Right now I am re-reading a book called *The Pursuit of God* by A.W. Tozer. It's *so* good! We read it last year in Master's Commission. I just finished reading chapter three, which is entitled "Removing the Veil." It talks about removing the veil in our hearts that keeps us from entering into God's presence; the veil is *ourself*, or the self-life. He goes on to say that if we want to get to that place of open communication with God, then we need to lay ourselves down like Christ did when He died on the cross, and that this laying down won't be pleasant. In fact, it will cause us a lot of pain and suffering. But that's what the Cross symbolizes. We need to be determined to truly allow this sanctifying work to be done in us, and it's only by surrendering our will to the leading of the Holy Spirit that we will experience new life in Christ.

This is what I want Lord—new life in You. Thank You for helping me to discern the truth from the lies. Thank You for helping me to surrender to the Holy Spirit more and more and be more successful at standing on Your truth. Thank You for helping me in my weakness, and confirming that I am *on the right path. You are so gracious and patient with me. I love you so much!*

Questions:

1. Have you ever had an emotional breakdown? If yes, when, why, and do you feel like you have received healing from it?

2. Is there anything in your life that you are really struggling with that you feel like you have been in a constant battle with? If yes, write it down. Now ask God what you need to do to overcome it. Now think about how you will implement this into your life.

3. Is there anything in your life that you know God is asking you to give up, but you really don't want to? If yes, what is it, and why don't you want to give it up?

Chapter 26

(October 25, 2004)

I was really encouraged at church yesterday. First of all, my friend Natalie and I chatted for a bit, and I am always so encouraged after spending time with her (I've started attending the small group she leads and I love it!). Then, the message was exactly what I needed to hear and really gave me more clarity and peace about my current situation.

During Pastor Alex's talk, he said that whether or not we feel called to the foreign mission field, we are all called to be missionaries. He also said that if we want God to use us to do big things for Him, we need to be faithful with the little things. I'm going to try my best to keep these things in the forefront of my mind, especially each day that I go into work. Oh yeah, I got hired on as a waitress/hostess at P.F. Chang's where I had my interview that I mentioned earlier! It's cool because I really love Chinese food, but I'm not so excited to be working at a restaurant. Don't get me wrong! I'm *very* thankful to have a job. It just feels like I've taken several steps backward from where I was, and that I'm missing out on something bigger and more exciting. After hearing the message at church yesterday, though, I know this isn't true and that I'm exactly where God wants me to be right now—I just hope not for very long. P.S. I decided not to apply to be an intern with

Relevant Magazine, because it seems very clear on the application that you need to be a student at a university to even be considered.

Speaking of being a missionary, a couple of days ago I was telling Meredith about a conversation I had with a guy I work with about church. I told her how I invited him to the young adults' service at our church. After I got done telling her this, she enthusiastically said, "You're a missionary!" When she said this, it really witnessed with my spirit. It felt like a true statement about who I am or who I am meant to be, and I'm not just talking about being a "missionary wherever I am," I'm talking about being a missionary in a foreign country. This surprised me. I've pondered this idea before but I haven't thought about it in too much detail. I mean I *would* like to do some sort of mission work overseas. I'm not exactly sure what and how and when and where, though, so I will just tuck this away for now and trust that God will show me when I need to know.

Coincidentally, *if there is such a thing*, the first table I had on my very first night of work was a group of missionaries! I was feeling really overwhelmed that night and slightly depressed because I really wasn't excited about being there, and God sent me a group of missionaries! I ended up crying to one of the women at my table. I told her that I didn't want to be serving tables. I wanted to be out on the mission field like her. Her response was very encouraging. She said, "Don't worry. Your time will come. Just be patient." I know this wasn't just a coincidence. I know it was God letting me know that I was right where He wanted me to be, and He was reminding that He had great plans for me, but that I needed to be patient. He is so gracious, patient, and kind. Then the message at church this past Sunday was like a repeat of what God had just told me my first night of work. Lesson: I need to be faithful where I am and patient; trusting that God knows what He is doing and will help me and make sure that I don't miss Him.

Questions:

1. Is there something you want to be doing right now that you are not doing? If yes, what is it, and why do you think you are not doing it? What can you do to be faithful where you are and better prepare for the next step?

2. What is your idea of "missions"?

Chapter 27

(November 6, 2004)

Wow! Just wow! What an amazing night! Jesus revealed a lie to me that I was believing about myself—a lie that was the source of a lot of my struggles and frustrations in trying to move forward with Him.

Our session tonight was about the Cross and what it symbolizes. As part of the session, they had us all watch a clip from the movie *The Passion of the Christ*. It was the part of the movie where Jesus was carrying the cross. Before they played it, they encouraged us to meditate (while we watched the clip) on the fact that it was our sins that put Jesus there, and to not think about anyone else's sins but our own. I was a little apprehensive at first; nevertheless, I did my best to follow their instructions.

As I watched the clip, the thoughts that kept going through my head were, "Stop it! Stop it! You didn't do anything wrong. Just leave me. You don't deserve to go through this. I do. Just leave me." I couldn't stand the fact that I was part of the reason Jesus suffered so cruelly. I felt so ashamed. As I continued to watch the clip, the weight of my guilt got heavier and heavier until it was almost too much to bear.

Then, before my spirit was crushed beneath the weight, Jesus came to my rescue by filling me with the most amazing sense of love and acceptance that I've ever felt. Then He said something to me that pierced my heart, something I know I'll never forget. He said, "You are worth it! Even if you were the only person on the face of the earth that was living in sin, I would die this death all over again just for you. I love you that much and I could never and *would* never just leave you." Jesus was lovingly continuing to help me see myself how He sees me: not just a sinful human being, but a precious and dearly loved child of the Most High God.

As the clip ended, we sat in silence for a short time and Jesus continued to speak to me. He said that if I wanted to move forward with Him, it was critical for me to give Him my guilt and accept His love and forgiveness. I was blown away by the fact that Jesus was so passionate about me receiving His forgiveness for my sins. It's our human nature to continually remind other people of their guilt and to not forgive them. It's the nature of God to forgive. It's the nature of God to desire to restore relationship with us, no matter what we've done. It's what He lives for. It's what He died for.

The next exercise they had us do was to proceed to the front of the room in two lines and receive a huge nail, one that was similar in size to the ones that were used to nail Jesus to the cross. Then, after we received our nail, we were to walk under a big cross that was set up in the front left corner of the room. It symbolized the fact that our sins are covered under Jesus' blood that was shed on the cross. While waiting in line to receive my nail, I heard Jesus, in my mind, tell me that before I walked under the cross, He wanted me to say out loud with my mouth, "I am worth it." This was extremely difficult for me, firstly because I guess I didn't fully believe it, and secondly because it meant admitting that I played a part in nailing Jesus to the cross. I understood this in my head, but I had never dealt with it in my heart. I didn't want to face this ugly truth. I was obedient though. When I spoke the words, "I am worth it," I felt a heaviness lift off of me, which was immediately replaced by a newfound sense of peace and freedom. My eyes had been fully opened to my true value in God, and I had been set free from guilt.

I AM WORTH IT!!! I wanted to scream it from the rooftops. I wanted to shout it from the mountaintops. I AM WORTH IT!!! I AM WORTH IT!!!! I wanted to scream and shout, jump and dance, and laugh and cry—all at the same time. Deep down I was *hoping* this was true, and now I knew for a fact that it was. The first verse of "Amazing Grace" played in my mind:

> Amazing grace, how sweet the sound, that saved a wretch like me. I once was lost, but now I'm found. Was blind, but now I see.[10]

I see how much God loves me, and I receive His love. I am not defined by my sin, and as I continue to remember God's unconditional, sacrificial love for me, I will have the motivation and strength to overcome it and be who God created me to be: a mirror of Him.

After I accepted this truth, it gave me an even stronger desire to share this good news with others so that they can experience the same freedom, healing, and restored relationship with God as I have. We are all worth it! God loves us all *so* much. We are all precious to Him, but we need to make the choice to join our lives with Him through faith in and submission to Christ if we want to experience this liberated, healed, and restored relationship with God. Romans 5:1-2, 5-11 says:

> *Therefore, since we have been justified through faith, we have peace with God through our Lord Jesus Christ, through whom we have gained access by faith into this grace in which we now stand. And we boast in the hope of the glory of God...And hope does not put us to shame, because God's love has been poured out into our hearts through the Holy Spirit, who has been given to us. You*

see, at just the right time, when we were still powerless, Christ died for the ungodly. Very rarely will anyone die for a righteous person, though for a good person someone might possibly dare to die. But God demonstrates his own love for us in this: While we were still sinners, Christ died for us. Since we have now been justified by his blood, how much more shall we be saved from God's wrath through him! For if, while we were God's enemies, we were reconciled to him through the death of his Son, how much more, having been reconciled, shall we be saved through his life! Not only is this so, but we also boast in God through our Lord Jesus Christ, through whom we have now received reconciliation.

God to me:

Thank you for letting Me do this in you today. I know how much it hurt, and I know you are sorry. Remember, don't get caught up in the cares of this world. I have made you to be a mirror to reflect My love to people. You are doing good. Stay focused on Me. You are Mine. Lay down your failures and don't pick them up again. Remember, I've earned the right to take them.

Questions:

1. What does the Cross of Christ symbolize to you?

2. Do you have a hard time forgiving yourself? If yes, why? Do you feel that Christ's forgiveness is enough for you?

3. How does it make you feel to know that while you were yet a sinner, Christ died for you?

4. Listen to the song "Start Over" by Flame on the album "Royal Flush."

Chapter 28

(December 22, 2004)

So, it's been almost three months since I've arrived in Florida. This past month, I think I sort of forgot why I came here. Before I left, pastor David from Shepherd's Heart Church in Peebles prayed for me. He said he felt like God was getting ready to send me on a journey to learn how to hear His voice more. Well I must say, it's not as easy to hear God's voice here as it was last year in Master's Commission. Obviously there is a big difference between now and then. It's like I went from sitting in a quiet classroom with other soldiers, all different ranks, discussing plans of attack, to being placed right in the middle of a loud battlefield all alone. I know I'm not alone, but it feels like it most of the time. So far, I've won some battles and I've lost some. I have actually had some pretty rough battles lately, where I've failed to resist temptation in different areas and have taken some pretty bad hits, namely to my confidence and self-esteem. This has left me feeling weak. I know that God wants me to receive His forgiveness. It just scares me to think how easy it is for me to give into my flesh and lose my focus when things get hard. Not surprisingly, God has been faithful to (in one way or another) always direct my attention back to Him and His purposes, taking every opportunity to speak words of love, comfort, and healing. He's so amazing!

Thank You Lord for always directing my attention back to You and showering me with Your love. Even now I can feel my strength coming back, and I just know I am going to come back stronger. I know that all I need to do when I fall is come to You, repent, and receive Your forgiveness. You have shown me that I can start over like this because of what You did on the Cross. Thank You so much for Your sacrifice. I know that the only way that sin can have power over me is if I don't confess it and if I don't give my guilt to You. I know sometimes it's hard for me to receive Your grace, but I know that this is Your heart for me and the only path to true healing.

(December 28, 2004)

God to me:

> I need you to find your worth in Me. Remember, no one will ever be enough for you and you will never be enough for anyone. There are things you can offer and be for people, and this is important, but the things that you alone offer will fade and disappoint. You can't always be there for people, but I can. You see what I mean? You need to make more of an effort to put Me first. If you want to make a big impact for Me (and I know that you do) then you need to do this. Don't let fear of any kind hold you back. You will not be alone. You won't miss out. You must keep your eyes focused on Me. Don't let anything take your focus off of Me. If you take your focus off of Me, then you will fall, and I know you don't want to fall. I know you want to honor Me in everything. Following Me is not easy, remember? Now is not a time to take it easy, it is a time to fight. There are things

all around you trying to take your focus off of Me. Don't let them. (Hebrews 12:2; Proverbs 4:27).

Lord, thank You for reminding me again that nothing and no one will ever be enough to fill the void You've created inside of Me; a void that can only be filled by You. You deserve, more than anyone else, to be praised and admired. I admit that I am weak in this area. Thank You for protecting me though. Thank You for the desire You've placed inside of me to not give up in continuing to seek after You and love You more; to lay myself down and strive to always put You first.

(January 10, 2005)

A resonating message God has been speaking to me the past couple of months is, "It's okay to fall… just don't stay there." He's been reminding me that He knows I am not perfect and that I am only dust (Psalm 103:14). But I can't use this as an excuse to stop trying. I need to remember and truly embrace what He has given me in Christ (Ephesians 1:3), and I need to keep pressing "on toward the goal to win the prize for which God has called me heavenward in Christ Jesus" (Philippians 3:14). God has also been encouraging me to be quicker to confess my sin and let Him heal me so I can keep moving forward.

I am not my failures! I'm learning to overcome strongholds, I need to truly believe what God says about me, and not the lies the devil is speaking to me. I have such a hard time accepting God's abundant grace, but I know that I need to accept it if I want to continue to move forward in Him and His plans for me to help other people walk in this freedom.

I just *hate* that I've fallen back so much lately. God deserves so much more from me. I just need to rest in the fact that God knows my heart, and He will continue to help me become more and more like Him. He is so patient with me. I just need to learn to be more patient with myself, and I must never give up.

(January 15, 2005)

(Grace Walk Conference)

What impeccable timing this is. =)

Ok God, I hear you. I am covered by Your amazing grace.

A few notes from the conference:

Negative attitudes create negative moods. To change this, we must ask the Holy Spirit to reveal to us the times we are thinking negatively, or agreeing with the lies the devil is speaking to us. Then we need to mentally affirm truth in place of negativity or lies. Then we need to take an outward step to affirm the truth we are believing in.

Lord, teach me to think your thoughts.

God to me:

> Practice what you just wrote down =). My blessed child, rise up in My power. I am all around you. You are to be an example to others of how to worship Me in Spirit and in truth. I am very pleased with you. I know your heart rejoices in My truth, and that brings Me so much joy. My heart rejoices over you. I know the plans I have for you: plans to prosper you (Jeremiah. 29:11). It fills Me with so much joy that you are starting to really believe this now.

Questions:

1. Describe a time that you have fallen spiritually. Describe a time that you have overcome spiritually. What was the difference?

2. Is there any sin in your life that you haven't confessed? If yes, what is it?

3. Is there any sin in your life that you have already confessed that you still feel really guilty about? If yes, what is it? Now read Isaiah 1:18 and 1 John 1:8-9.

4. What do you think Ephesians 1:3 means when it says that God has blessed us in the heavenly realms with every spiritual blessing in Christ?

5. Write down some of the negative labels people have given you and that you have given yourself. Include any negative thoughts that come into your mind about yourself when you have made a mistake. For example, "lazy, stupid, selfish." Now read 2 Corinthians 5:21 and write down what you think this means, especially in reference to the negative labels you've written down.

6. Think of a time you were in a negative mood. Now ask the Holy Spirit to reveal to you why you were in a negative mood. Write it down. Now ask the Holy Spirit to reveal to you any lies you might be believing about yourself, another person, or God. Now, mentally affirm truth in place of these lies.

7. What do you think Galatians 5:1 means when it says, "It is for freedom that Christ has set us free. Stand firm, then, and do not let yourselves be burdened again by a yoke of slavery"?

Chapter 29

(January 24, 2005)

I am struggling, Lord.

God to me:

My child, keep putting up a fight. Be strong! Don't stop fighting until you break through! I am teaching you an important lesson. A lesson you need to learn. I am allowing you to experience feelings of frustration and distance to teach you how much you need Me. I am the one who lifts up. I am the one who puts those who are broken back together again. Everything that is good comes from Me (James 1:17).

(February 5, 2005)

God to me:

Don't focus on what you don't have. Focus on what you do have. Your life is a lush garden. Yes, there are weeds that need to be pulled out, but you see how you can miss out on the beauty all around you if you just focus on the weeds and how ugly they are. Yes, they are ugly, but the beauty is much more. Only focusing on the weeds is not going to help you. It will only discourage you and keep you from moving forward. Jesus had the strength to die on the cross because He focused on the joy set before Him (Hebrews 12:2). Stay focused on Me and let Me be your joy. As long as you keep seeking Me, your eyes will continue to open more and more and My light will shine brighter and brighter through you. You know what My footprints look like. Follow them.

(February 19, 2005)

God to me:

I am always with you, always working, always moving. There will be a time for you to rest, but not now. Keep fighting. Keep pressing forward. I will carry you. I can hold you. Trust me!

(March 29, 2005)

Dear Jesus, You are good enough for me. In fact You are more than enough for me. Sorry I haven't been acting like it lately. You are all-knowing, all-powerful, and all-present (Psalm 139:1-18; Psalm 147:5; Isaiah 40:28). You know what You're doing. I don't. I need You. I need You so bad. Thank You for not letting me be satisfied with anything or anyone else but You. You make sense to me. I am lost without You. Please help me to stay focused on You and what You are doing. I need direction. I want to be where You are. I am feeling so sad and lost right now.

God to me:

My dear, dear, precious child. I love you so much, and there is nothing you can do that will separate you from My love. I will never give up on you. Please believe Me. Hold onto Me. Take My hand and you will see that I will be there to guide you. Make prayer your focus. Make growing in truth a priority. Do not look to the right or to the left (Proverbs 4:27). All you will find outside of Me is confusion. Listen to Me. Trust Me. It is a battle, and you are a very real target (1 Peter 5:8). I know you are starting to learn just how true this is. It's time for you to take your position. DO YOU HEAR ME? It is time for you to take your stand against the devil's schemes (Ephesians 6:10-11). Stand on My Word. Don't be afraid to commit. You've walked the line long enough. Don't worry, I will make sure you get to where you need to go. You need to keep taking steps towards Me. I won't let you miss Me. Regardless of what you decide to do, you will be a slave. You will either be a slave to sin or a slave to righteousness (Romans 6:16). Give yourself to righteousness. Whatever you need to give up will not be worth the prize you will receive when you choose Me. Practical steps need to be taken on your part. If you are not sure what to do, do what you think I would do. Water that ceases to flow becomes stagnant. Flow, my sweet child, and allow Me to carry you on.

(May 3, 2005)

God to me:

> HOLD ON! I am setting the stage for something awesome, as crazy as that might sound to you right now, and as much as it feels like the total opposite. YOU ARE MINE! Mine. I hear your cries.

(May 8, 2005)

God to me:

> You know My Word is true. Hold fast. "As Scripture says, 'Anyone who believes in him will never be put to shame'" (Romans 10:11).

Lord, thank You for being my ever present help in times of need (Psalm 46:1), which has been a lot lately. Thank You for always being right beside me, preserving me. You are worthy of all my trust and love and life. Thank You for Your encouragement, promises, and patience. You are so wonderful! I just want to be a light for You, and even though I'm struggling so much at doing this, I don't want to give up. Please help me. Amen

(May 11, 2005)

Thank You, Lord, for continuing to purify me. Thank You for leading me here. I have really struggled in this place, but You are worth it to me. I know You are doing a great work in me, and I want You to finish it. I feel so safe in Your arms. I'm glad I know You the way I do. Thank You for being my sight when I can't see. Thank You for stirring my heart when I feel lifeless. Thank You for calling me Your child and putting Your Holy Spirit in me. Thank You for not letting me be satisfied with anything less than Your good, pleasing, and perfect will for me. I love You so much. Thank You for not letting me go crazy, which I feel like I've been dangerously close to lately. Thank You for always believing in me, protecting me, and rescuing me time and time again. You always come through for me. Amen

God to me:

> It is with eager expectation that I wait to reveal My plans to you. You will be so pleased. Everything is going to be okay. I know it hurts right now. I know you can't see down the road, and that makes you feel nervous. I know that sometimes you feel like you are just so far behind. But trust Me when I say,"You are not." I'm doing a great work in you.

Questions:

1. Can you remember a time where you felt frustrated and distant from God? If yes, how did you get through it?

2. What do you think was "the joy set before Jesus" that helped Him endure the cross (Hebrews 12:2)?

3. Does God love *everyone* and want them to come to repentance, or just a few people? Refer to 2 Peter 3:9.

4. In your own words, what do you think Paul was talking about when he said in Philippians 4:12 that he has learned to be content in all things?

5. When it comes to your life in general, are you still "in control" or have you let Jesus take control? If you are still mostly "in control," what areas or things in your life have you refused to let Jesus have control or lordship over?

6. Do you truly believe that God is trustworthy and that He has great plans for you (Jeremiah 29:11)?

Chapter 30

(May 20, 2005)

So, I just ended an unhealthy dating relationship that I was in for three months! This explains why I have been struggling so much over the past three months. Part of me is hesitant to even write about this, because it was such an incredibly low point for me. I failed myself and God *a lot* while in this relationship, and I obviously don't deal well with failure. One way that I tend to deal with really hard problems, or areas where I'm struggling to trust God, is to deny their existence. God has been teaching me that this is very unhealthy, and that I need to deal with these obstacles head on if I want to overcome them. Another part of me is excited to write about this, because it is such a powerful testimony of God's unconditional love and faithfulness.

I knew before I moved to Orlando that it would be a place where I would have to trust God a lot more, and I willingly welcomed this challenge. Since the beginning of my walk with Christ, it's been a prayer of mine that my faith in Jesus would only get increasingly stronger. I knew that moving to Orlando would be difficult, but I did it anyway because I had complete faith that Jesus was going to help me through it. I definitely didn't expect this move to result in me falling into so much sin. God knew that it would, though, and I am so thankful that He graciously taught me how to completely receive His forgiveness so that I wouldn't become overwhelmed with despair and give up all together. God is so good!!!

So now, I'm going to write down some pertinent details about this relationship, and then share the understanding that the Holy Spirit has given me about why I entered into this relationship in the first place, why it took me so long to end it, and how I can be more successful at avoiding this same kind of mistake in the future.

I met my now ex-boyfriend in early February while working at Chamberlin's, a health food store where I worked part-time for several months. From the moment I met him at the checkout counter, I felt an unusually strong attraction to him. I could tell that he was attracted to me as well. As I rang up his groceries, we had a nice little chat and, to my delight, he ended up giving me his phone number and telling me to call him sometime. I say "to my delight" because, at the time, I was feeling lonely, frustrated, and discouraged with where I was at in life; this attention, affection, and feeling of "happiness" was a very welcome change. I know these negative emotions caused me to be very vulnerable, and I should have been more guarded. I also know that God wanted to be enough for me. This is probably why He was letting me feel these negative emotions so strongly. He wanted me to run into *His* arms for comfort, not anyone else's.

After I got off work that day, I asked God if it was okay if I called him. I couldn't make out a clear "yes" or "no," and instead of waiting for a clear confirmation and asking my close friends and spiritual leaders for advice, I went ahead and called him. Not surprisingly, things progressed too quickly between us and it wasn't long before we became an official couple.

I know that the reason I was struggling to make out a clear answer was *not* because God hadn't given me one. I remember that when I first locked eyes with my boyfriend, *before we even spoke,* the word "lust" popped into my mind. I know now that from that moment I should have kept my distance from him. It wasn't what I wanted to hear though, so I didn't listen. That was the first instance in the relationship that I gave into the desires of my flesh. Shortly after we met, before we became an official couple, I became aware of the fact that he wasn't a Christian. There were a few other signs that made it pretty clear that I shouldn't have entered into a dating relationship with him. I foolishly ignored them.

So why did it take me so long to end this relationship?

Like I mentioned, this relationship ended up lasting for about three months, which of course was three months too long. I believe it took me so long to end the relationship because I was continually grieving the Holy Spirit, doing what I knew I shouldn't. As a result, I was weak and confused. God never abandoned me though, and I finally decided to listen and get out. I have learned through this experience that sin can make its way into our lives very subtly at first; then suddenly we can find ourselves tangled up in the rather large, sticky web of sin, and it will be very hard to get out. Toward the end of the relationship, I actually had a dream that I was tangled up in a really thick, sticky web, and I knew it was God warning me to get out.

I know that I cannot live a life of faith in my own strength. Jesus has reminded me over and over that I need to remain in Him, especially when times are tough (John 15:5). I didn't realize how strong-willed I was. By the end of this relationship, I had drifted very far away from Jesus through my disobedience, and I desperately missed the close fellowship I used to have with Him. In fact, I yearned for it. It took me about three months of being in this relationship to accept the fact that I couldn't live my way and God's way at the same time. I had to make a choice. If I wanted to live big for God, I needed to trust Him and honor Him with every area of my life—even when it's *really* hard. This is the true test of faith.

Another reason I didn't end the relationship sooner was because I didn't want to hurt my boyfriend. He had already experienced so much hurt and heartache in his life, and I didn't want to add to that. To cause others pain is very against my nature, but I've learned that just being nice to someone to keep their feelings from being hurt might end up enabling them to remain in their broken state, which is not what I want either. I want to help people find healing and wholeness. The only way that I can really help someone find true healing and wholeness is to lead them to Christ, and the best way to do that is to *live out* my faith. In this instance, I wasn't being a very good witness.

I've learned that sometimes, following God's Spirit means letting go of someone or telling someone something they don't want to hear, possibly causing them pain, and I have to be okay with that. They might hurt for a little bit, but hopefully it will cause them to draw closer to God (2 Corinthians 7:8-11). Yet, even if they don't, that isn't my responsibility. My responsibility is to follow God's leading.

So, how can I avoid making this same mistake in the future?

I have learned that repentance, prayer, and praise is vital in helping us experience victory over our sinful nature. I have also learned that repentance, prayer, and praise *alone* is not enough! We need to read the Bible! Having a good working knowledge of the Bible will help us to be more effective in our time spent with God. I have struggled to read my Bible on a regular basis from the time I first surrendered my heart to the Lord. This really says something to me. If reading the Bible wasn't such a powerful weapon against the enemy, then there wouldn't be such a battle inside trying to prevent me from reading it. I know I'm not the only one who struggles with this.

I know that when I read my Bible on a regular basis, I am a lot more successful at doing what it says, and I feel a lot closer to Jesus. The two go hand in hand because they are one and the same

(John 1:1; Revelations 19:13)! I have heard people say on many occasions that Jesus is in every book of the Bible. I have also heard that the Bible is the complete revelation of Jesus Christ (who is the complete revelation of the Father)! How cool is that?! It makes so much sense to me. In John 14:6, Jesus refers to Himself as, "The way, the truth, and the life," and John 8:32 says, "Then you will know the truth, and the truth will set you free." 1 Corinthians 10:13 says, "No temptation has overtaken you except what is common to mankind. And God is faithful; he will not let you be tempted beyond what you can bear. But when you are tempted, he will also provide a way out so that you can endure it." As I have read and studied the Bible, it's become very clear to me that Jesus is our way out! We need to stand on the truth of who He is and who we are in Him.

Hebrews 12:1-2 says, "Therefore, since we are surrounded by such a great cloud of witnesses, let us throw off everything that hinders and the sin that so easily entangles. And let us run with perseverance the race marked out for us, ***fixing our eyes on Jesus,*** the pioneer and perfecter of our faith. For the joy set before him he endured the cross, scorning its shame, and sat down at the right hand of the throne of God." Jesus is the "pioneer and perfecter of our faith." It makes sense that we need to fix our eyes on Him to be successful at living a life of faith. Now when I say that you should read the Bible, I don't mean just read it so you can check off that you've read it. Read it for the sake of understanding who Jesus is, and how you should respond to that knowledge.

If I do end up entering into sin, I need to repent right away and hold fast to the truth that I am forgiven (Isaiah 1:18; 1 John 1:8-9). I say this, because it is one of Satan's strategies to try to make us continue to feel guilty even after we have repented. I know I definitely struggle with this, but I also know I'm not the only one. This guilt often leads to further sin, thus beginning a dangerous downward spiral. We need to remember that Jesus earned the right to take the guilt of our sin, and His grace is sufficient for us.

If Jesus says we are forgiven, WE ARE FORGIVEN (1 John 1:9)! God doesn't want us to wallow in self-pity and guilt. He wants us to receive His forgiveness, cling to Christ once again, and press on towards the goal for which God has called us heavenward in Christ Jesus (Philippians 3:1-12).

Also an important note: we don't need to get our act together before we run to God. In fact, when we are deeply entrenched in sin is when we need to run to God the most. He is our only way out, and He wants to help us! He is rich in mercy and loving kindness (Psalm 86:5, 15; Psalm 145:8; Ephesians 2:4-5). He will never turn anyone away who comes to Him in humility and brokenness, asking for His help—*no matter what they've done.* Not a single one of us deserves this kind of love, but God freely gives it to all who will humble themselves and call upon His name (Romans 10:13).

When I finally decided to end my unhealthy dating relationship, God didn't make me feel bad. I guess He knew I felt bad enough. Among other things, He told me how proud He was of me for trusting Him and laying this relationship down. I was yet again in awe of the amazing, gracious, unfailing love of God.

Here is what God spoke to me at church the night that I decided to officially end this relationship:

God to me:

> Today was a great victory! I told you that I would not let you be satisfied with anything less than My best for you. I love you so much! I know you love Me too. Thank you for proving your love to Me today. You are going to be so delighted that you chose to trust Me with this. I know just how much faith and trust you are putting in Me, and that is **so** beautiful to Me. You are becoming less, and I am becoming more. I know that you

> can only see in part. If you could see perfectly like Me, things would be easier; but you can't, and yet still you choose Me. I told you I would help you choose Me. Breathe… I will take care of you. You won't miss out. You are completely safe in My arms. In fact, in My arms is the safest place you could ever be. Through your actions today, you have proven that you're really starting to believe this. As far as your next couple of steps, I am preparing things and people for you. It's all good. I love your hunger. Fear not, you will have a bounty. You are starting to see more clearly that you are Mine! MINE! I am jealous for you (Exodus 20:4-5). I love you so much! And I know you love me too.

Since I've moved to Florida, God has shown me just how much I need Him *every minute of everyday*, and I feel like He has been allowing everything that I claim to believe in to be put to the test (1 Peter 1:6-8). During this process, He has been so gracious and has told me over and over again that I need to trust Him and put Him first. I didn't realize how stubborn I was and how many areas in my heart weren't surrendered to Him. Like a child with a parent, I was really testing my limits. This has truly been a very humbling and cleansing experience. I am not saying I have arrived, but I feel like I've come a *long* way.

Dear God, I can't thank you enough for rescuing me like You did. Thank You for being faithful to help me become more like You. Thank You that You are turning this around for Your good (Romans 8:28). I love You so much!

Questions:

1. What does it mean to "grieve the Holy Spirit"?

2. What is the definition of "repent"?

3. Are you living in any blatant or unrepentant sin? If yes, what is it, and why are you living in it?

4. Do you have any unconfessed sin in your life (something you are not necessarily doing now, but you haven't confessed and dealt with)? What is it? It is important that you deal with this somehow, so that the devil can't use it to keep you in bondage.

5. What is your idea of "setting boundaries" in a dating or friendship relationship?[11]

6. Do you have someone in your life that you can talk to about things you are struggling with, someone who can help keep you accountable and help you work through difficult things? **Remember: Don't struggle alone.**

7. Where are your weak spots (what makes you vulnerable to sin)?

8. What are some things that really spoke to you from this chapter?

Chapter 31

(May 26, 2005)

I have been up and down a lot lately. I feel like I'm at a crossroads, and I need to make a serious decision about the direction I want my life to go. Am I going to totally trust God and live a radical, sold out life for Jesus; or will I take the safe and easy road? I know that ending the unhealthy dating relationship I was in was a huge step in the right direction. I am just at a loss as to what my next step should be. I'm feeling really restless where I'm at, which makes me think that I'm not meant to stay here. I'm trying my best to trust that God will continue to make clear to me the direction I'm supposed to take. Until then, I'm just going to try my best to be faithful where I am.

I've been in Florida for a little over seven months now, and I have been unemployed for the past two months. In order to pay my bills, I've been doing random side jobs. My ex-boyfriend helped me out some while we were together as well. I left Chamberlain's because I was starting to feel trapped there, and when I prayed about it, I had peace about leaving. However, it didn't take very long for me to realize that my work situation needed to become more stable.

As soon as I came to this realization, I started working really hard to finish everything required to get my Florida massage license, and I'm happy to say, I've finally completed everything!

I probably won't be able to get a job doing massage until July though. I don't know why I put this off for so long. Oh well, God has helped me get by up to this point, and I just have to trust He will continue to bring me jobs until I can get hired on at a spa or something similar. Part of me feels like God has more than massaging for me. But like I said earlier, I have no clue what that might be, so I'm just going to keep my eyes out for a nice place to work as a massage therapist unless He directs me otherwise.

Sermon notes from this morning at Church in the Son:

We always have a choice. To live by the truth or not. Brokenness is good. It breaks down our own strong will and helps us to align ourselves with the Lord. When we turn from God, we lose the power of the Holy Spirit in our lives. The anointing is fragile. The enemy is subtle and deceptive. We need to make time to get alone with God. The enemy tries to convince us to spare ourselves. He tries to get us to take the easy road of compromise. Truth will follow us and keep knocking on our door though. God wants to make His word alive to us. God's Word will change us (Proverbs 23:23). We need to get rid of our idols and humble ourselves and move to a deeper level of obedience.

Wow! It's amazing how much this sermon exactly describes what I just went through and what God has been teaching me through it all!

Thank You Lord for Your love and faithfulness! I want to be so consumed with You that, "For to me, to live is Christ and to die is gain" (Philippians 1:21).

(June 6, 2005)

Today was an AMAZING day! It was a real spiritual breakthrough for me, and I am yet again in awe of the awesome love of God.

I went to visit a church called Rejoice Christian Fellowship, which is a small, non-denominational church in Orlando. The service was at the pastor's house because they were baptizing people in his pool afterward, and then having a potluck. From the moment I walked in the door to the moment I left (seven hours), I felt God's presence. It was so wonderful. I had really missed and yearned for this kind of close fellowship with God, and I was extremely thankful to have it for such an extended period of time. It took everything in me to not be a ball of tears the entire time. It was like the whole service and day was planned out just for me, for my healing.

The service lasted for about an hour and a half. We sang a lot of old songs, most of which were among some of the first praise and worship songs I ever learned. It really brought me back. Then, when the pastor spoke, it was like God was speaking directly to me, and I somehow managed to only let a few tears escape. I was glad, because I didn't want to lose it in front of a bunch of people I had just met.

Ever since I moved to Florida, I have been struggling with bouts of anxiety and depression. But for the past couple of weeks, I've really gotten serious about surrendering my anxious thoughts to God and declaring His promises for me; I've determined in my heart that I'm not going to give up on living a radical, sold out life for Jesus. Today, God let me know that I've passed the test. He said that He saw that I was determined to trust Him even though it was really hard and I was really afraid, and because I trusted Him in this way, a more powerful anointing to do great things for Him was coming my way. When God spoke this to me, it raised my level of faith. God said He would help me, and He did!

Sermon notes from Rejoice Christian Fellowship today:

God is never doing nothing. We need to LOOK UP! There is a reason God calls us to uncomfortable situations. It is to purify our faith and test us to find out if we are going to really trust Him or not. If we don't trust God, then we don't get the new thing. We have to go through the discomfort with the right attitude, trusting Jesus and looking up. It will always be worth it.

God to me:

> Oh, My child, this is only the beginning. You are on the right path. You are radical. You've passed! I see that you really trust Me.

After feeling like a major failure for the past several months, these words meant more to me than I can say. I am so full of joy and excitement right now, I feel like I'm going to BURST!

Dearest Lord, Thank You for filling my heart so full today. My cup overflows (Psalm 23:5). You are so faithful and worthy of all my praise. I DO trust You. Thank You for making that very evident to me today. I am so blessed and its all because of You Lord. Its because of You that I have been able to overcome. You are my refuge and strength. You are my strong tower (Psalm 18:2, 59:9, 61:3, 62:7, 91:2).

Questions:

1. Is there anything you are anxious about regarding your future? If yes, write it down and write a prayer of thanks to God for how He is going to take care of it and you.

2. Ask God what it would look like for you to live a radical, sold out life for Him, right now. Write down what He says. Note: don't make any big decisions until you have prayed a lot about it and talked to a trusted leader and received advice and counsel. If the answer is still yes after this, then GO FOR IT!

3. Write your definition of "complete trust."

4. Would you describe your relationship with God as close and intimate? If your answer is no, then write down some things you could do to change this.

5. Are you struggling with anxiety or depression right now? If you are struggling with anxiety look up Philippians 4:6-7. After you have read it, write down everything you are feeling anxious about. After you have completed this list, write down a prayer telling God what you need. Then thank Him for how He is going to help you. If you are struggling with depression, look up Psalm 43:5. Now write down all the reasons you are feeling low. Now read Psalm 55:22 and 1 Peter 5:7 and, in written words, cast your cares upon the Lord.

Additional helpful scriptures for depression: Isaiah 26:3-4; Romans 15:13; 2 Peter 2:9.

Chapter 32

(June 29, 2005)

Well, a lot of significant things have happened in my life since the last time I've written. First of all, I went to visit my family in Ohio a few weeks ago. Liz and I had come up with the plan to go home and surprise Dad for his birthday and Father's Day. I flew from Orlando to Boston, where Liz is still living, and we drove to Ohio from there.

We arrived in Bellevue at 11 p.m. on Tuesday night. Dad was still up sitting in his chair watching TV, and we sure surprised him alright! It couldn't have been more perfect. The expression of surprise and joy on his face was priceless. After he realized that it was actually Liz and I standing there, he said in a surprised, joyous tone, "My girls are home!"

We were home for exactly one week. It was really nice being home, even though there were some rough moments. Some problems my parents have been having in their relationship are really starting to come to the surface. They are empty nesters now, which I've heard can really test a marriage. It seems like they are communicating much more, which is a good thing (I think).

I got to spend some time with Cathy in Bellevue and also in Toledo where she is now living and going to nursing school! It was really nice. I have really missed her. When we were together we talked a lot about old times and about the future: mainly how we want to have wonderful husbands and kids and be neighbors just like when we were kids.

I would *love* to settle down right beside her, but it all depends on if it is part of God's plan for me. That's the most important thing to me. I don't say this lightly. I say it knowing that to follow God's will means that it will most definitely cost me some things that are very dear to me. In regards to this, I have a feeling, which is hard for me to ignore, that Cathy and I might have very different paths and we most likely won't be neighbors. If this is the case, I know it will really hurt, but I have to trust that God knows best.

Liz and I got to spend a lot of time with our sweet little nephew Caleb (Michael's son) while we were home. He is so cute, I can hardly stand it! He's talking a mile a minute about everything under the sun. He's a very affectionate and loving little boy, well behaved for the most part, and seems very happy. This makes my heart happy.

By the time Liz and I were getting ready to leave, we were all just getting used to being around each other again. It was hard to leave. Oddly enough, I was excited to return to Florida, though. I wasn't sure why, because even though I just had a major spiritual breakthrough there, it still felt very much like a battleground, nothing near the comfort and security of being with my family. I knew God must have been up to something, and He was. Read on...

Before Liz and I left, we stopped by CVS so we could give Janet one last hug. Things with her and her boyfriend are not going well, and while we were there she ended up breaking down and crying to us about it. She is not one to cry very often, so I knew she must really be struggling. I hate this for her. Even though it was a sad time, it was also a special bonding time for us as sisters, and I cherished it greatly.

Speaking of special sister bonding time, the drive to Boston went really well. I drove until a little after midnight, then Liz took over driving duty. Before we got back on the road, we walked around the parking lot for a little bit to stretch our legs and try to wake up. Then, I don't know if it was the tiredness (which can sometimes bring out our goofy sides) or what, but we proceeded to chase each other around Liz's car a couple of times. We giggled like little girls. It was great fun! Then, to end our delightful time of childish fun, we played hide and seek. With the car in between us, we took turns popping our heads up in the car window and quickly ducking down as soon as we caught a glimpse of each other.

Just like I would have loved to stay in Ohio a little while longer, I would have loved to stay in Boston with Liz a little while longer. But like I said earlier, I was actually excited to get back to Florida. I know now that it was my spirit that was excited, because God was getting ready to open up a new door of great promise for me.

Now, what I am about to tell you next is the catalyst for the most recent (not to mention very welcome) major change in my life—the moment a new door of great promise began to open. It is also an awesome testimony to God's faithfulness.

On the plain ride home from Boston to Orlando, I ended up sitting across the aisle from a young guy from England named Stephen. Early on in our journey, I noticed that the word "MASTERS" was printed in bold letters on the book he was reading, along with the names of some books of the Bible. I asked him about it, and was very excited to learn that it was a training manual for Master's Commission! Coincidence? I think not.

When he started talking about Master's Commission, a flood of emotion rushed over me as I remembered with fondness my first year of the program. I told him that I did a year of Master's Commission in Ohio, and that I loved it! It felt so good to talk about it again, like a part of me that was dead had come back to life. The desire to pursue full-time ministry popped into the forefront of my mind, and very real feelings of hope were starting to rise up in me. Maybe, just maybe, it might still be in the cards for me. I say this because I thought I had journeyed too far off the path God had for me through bad decisions I had made since I moved to Florida, and that I had forfeited God's best for me, resulting in me having to settle for a lesser dream. Now what that lesser dream actually was, I wasn't sure. I knew that God still loved me, I was thankful for that, and I had made my peace with my lost dream of full-time ministry. But I soon found out that God didn't want me to make my peace with it. He wanted me to fight for it. He wanted me to know that He hadn't disqualified me. I had disqualified myself, and I had no right to do that. God also wanted me to know that He was holding my position if I wanted it. It was amazing how He revealed all of this to me. I will explain in more detail later.

I know that Satan played a big part in me believing I was disqualified. I know this is exactly what he wanted me to believe. Why did he want me to believe this lie? Well, I believe he wanted me to believe this lie because he knew it would keep me from pursuing God's best for me and being used by God to advance His Kingdom. I believe that many people give up on God's best for them because they don't fully understand the principles of grace and forgiveness. This is so sad to me, and I want to do all I can to stop it from happening.

For as long as I've been in Orlando, I haven't made any effort to look for a Master's Commission school here. I guess in the beginning I thought that Master's Commission wasn't in the plans for me any more, as I knew that I wasn't supposed to do a second year at Reality MC. I had forgotten about the dream I had when I was praying about whether I should go back for that second year. In the dream, I was planning on going to school, but the school looked far away in the distance. I understood this to mean that I wasn't supposed to go to school right away. I guess after I moved to Florida, I got caught up in the cares of life and forgot about the school part. As I thought about it, I knew that if I ended up doing a second year of Master's Commission that full-ti ministry would be part of my future. I know this isn't the with everyone that does a second year of Master's Commissi just knew that this would be the case for me.

As Stephen and I continued to talk, I found out that just completed his first year as a Master's Commission at a church in Southport, England, and that he was on his way to Orlando to observe a Master's school at a church called Faith Assembly of God. He was doing this in order to gain some helpful tips on how to lead a successful Master's Commission program back in England.

When Stephen told me the name of the church he would be visiting, I got even more excited, because I knew right where it was! During our conversation, I didn't have any intentions of enrolling as a second year MC student there. Like I said, at the time I didn't think I was qualified. My initial intention was to visit the church and meet some of the MC students and staff. I figured I could help volunteer at some events and hang out with them on occasion. I finally decided to check out the school last Tuesday.

Now from the time I met Stephen to the time I visited the church on Tuesday, God asked me several times why I wasn't pursuing full-time ministry. This surprised me. I couldn't believe that God would still trust me with this huge responsibility after the very poor choices I had made over the past several months.

I pondered this question, but I didn't think too hard about it, because I was well on my way to getting a job as a massage therapist. In fact, I had already interviewed at a nice spa and they wanted me to come back for a second interview! Then, on the following Monday during my morning walk, God was *really* building me up. He was telling me how beautiful He thought my heart was, how much He believed in me, and how much He delighted in my willingness to listen to Him and follow where He leads me—even when it's really hard. Then, what I heard Him say next made me understand why He was building me up so much.

What He was getting ready to ask me to do would take a lot of courage, not to mention confidence in my ability to trust in Him. He asked in an encouraging sort of tone, "Why not Master's?" Now, by God asking me this, it was like He was saying to me that I *wasn't* disqualified; that my dream of full-time ministry was in fact, not lost. This was deeply healing for me. It meant that I had been given a second chance at fulfilling my hearts deepest desire—to live big for God. I thought I had forfeited this dream, but apparently I hadn't. *God was helping me to understand grace at an even deeper level.*

As I was walking home trying to wrap my head around all of this, a man riding on a bicycle looked at me and said, "Keep it up! You've got it in you!" It was an almost surreal moment. I knew that God had sent that man to confirm (just in case doubt tried to creep it's way in) that I had in fact heard from Him, and that I was supposed to attend a second year of Masters—eventually pursuing full-time ministry. This wasn't the only confirmation that morning, either!

When I was almost home, God reminded me of a dream I had not long ago. In my dream, I was looking from an aerial view at a very large, tall corn field. In the middle of the corn field, I saw a vegetable garden full of all sorts of brightly colored, lush vegetables. I realized I was looking at it from an aerial view because I wouldn't have been able to see the garden from the ground, as the corn was so tall. Then I saw myself walking down a dirt lane, at the end of which stood a farmer. As I got closer to the farmer, I could see that he was very upset. I asked him why he was so upset, and he said (through tears), "She thinks it's gone, but I saved it for her. They tried to plow it down and plant corn in its place, but I saved it for her. I want her to have it, but she thinks it's gone." Then, after a moment of solemn silence, the farmer was surrounded by a bright light and had the appearance of a king, *and I turned into a princess!*

I knew then that the farmer was really God speaking to me, then I woke up. As I asked God what this dream meant, He revealed to me that the corn field represented the lies the devil was speaking to me (that I had messed up too bad and had forfeited God's best for my life), and the garden represented His plan for my life (full-time ministry and living big for Him). HE SAVED IT FOR ME! The devil was trying to convince me that it was gone and that it was all my fault. He was also trying to get me to conform to the ways of the world so I wouldn't stand out for God. I couldn't, through my own natural eyes, see the truth because the stalks of corn (the lies I was believing) were hiding it from me.

Seeing it from an aerial view in my dream represented God opening my spiritual eyes so that I could see what He saw—the truth. What is so beautiful and encouraging to me about all of this is that God knew my heart all along. He knew how desperately I wanted to trust Him and live for Him. Even more beautiful, He didn't hold my shortcomings against me. He helped me work through them! So nothing was lost. I only gained a deeper level of faith and intimacy with Jesus. God is *so* good, and *so* faithful!

God to me:

(Written after I returned from my walk)

> Know this, because there will be times that doubt will show it's ugly face… You have heard from Me! You have been faithful with a little, therefore I am getting ready to expand your territory. I am also getting ready to give you a greater freedom in Me. You will know what it's like to soar in the Spirit. You will know more of My presence. The seeds of faith you have planted in obedience will sustain you in the times to come, just as My Word does not return to Me void (Isaiah 55:11). I know that

> change takes getting used to, and sometimes you wish that I wouldn't ask you to change so much. Thank you for being obedient, though. Thank you for presenting yourself to Me as a willing vessel for Me to accomplish My purposes through. Keep seeking Me. Remember, the righteous will enjoy the fruit of their labor (Isaiah 3:10) and,"There is a time for everything, and a season for every activity under heaven" (Ecclesiastes 3:1). Now is a time for seeking, for I have much in store for you. There will be times I will call you to action, and there will be times when I call you to rest and be still. I know you have a heart to serve. I gave that to you for a reason. I know you have so many questions, but believe Me when I say you are on the right path. Keep seeking Me. You know you can trust Me and that I won't let you miss Me. Remember My faithfulness. I love you so much.

The next morning was Tuesday, and I was supposed to give my friend Donna a massage. She never came to the door, though, so I decided to go visit the church because it was right across the road from her house! I was still a little anxious about the whole idea of doing a second year of Master's, but I wasn't about to let that fear hold me back. I knew better than to do that. I walked around the main church building for a while, just taking it all in (it was a big building). Then, I asked someone in the main office where I could find the Master's Commission department. They directed me to the youth building around back. When I got there, I talked to the secretary of the school for a little while. We had a really good conversation, during which time I shared my testimony with her and told her how I ended up in Florida. After I finished sharing, she told me a little bit about the school and answered some questions I had about it. I walked out with a brochure and application. Before I left, Geni (the secretary) said I could call or come back anytime during regular office hours if I had any more questions, or just wanted to chat. Everything about it felt so right; like I was finally coming home after being lost for a while.

I went back the next day to try to get a better picture of what it would look like for me to be a second year Master's student there. I ended up attending the youth service that night, because I learned that as a Master's student there, I would be expected to be a youth leader. I was really impressed with everything I had learned about the school and the church up to that point, and it got me even more excited about the potential of being a second year student there. The following day, I had lunch with some people on staff at the school, including Geni. I felt so comfortable around all of them, like I'd known them for a while. I turned in my application the following day.

Questions:

1. Do you think you have messed up too bad, and in so doing have settled for a lesser dream or calling? If yes, ask God if this is what He is saying to you, or if you are believing a lie. Write down your conversation with God.

2. Is God asking you to make any sort of changes in your life in order to move forward in His plans for you? If yes, write them down. Also, write down any fears you might have about making these changes. Now, read all of the following portions of Scripture and write down what you have learned in regard to trusting God with your fears: Psalms 34:1-11, 55:22; Matthew 6:25-34; Luke 12:22-26; Philippians 4:4-11; 1 Peter 5:6-7.

Chapter 33

(July 3, 2005)

I went to Rejoice Christian Fellowship again this morning, and I am *so* glad I did! It was just as amazing as it was the first time I went. Again, when Pastor Rick spoke it was like God speaking directly to me, continuing to bring more healing to my heart, more clarity to all the confusion that has been going on in me since I moved to Florida, and more courage and strength to continue pressing forward into the things I know He has called me to do.

Dear Lord, I am in awe of the way You have been so faithful to me. I love You so much! You are in control more than I realize. I know that now. You are big enough to cover me if I mess up. I know that now. Thank You for how You have so lovingly guided me. I know I needed to go through what I did so I could become aware of the areas in my heart that weren't fully surrendered to You, learning even more of just how much I need You and how much You love me (Psalm 54:4; John 15:5).

(July 14, 2005)

I had my interview for Masters Commission today, and it went really well! The girl that interviewed me said that I should hear back in the next couple of days about whether or not I've been accepted.

(July 16, 2005)

Ahh!! I'm in!!! I got the call today that I have been accepted to be a second year student at Orlando Master's Commission! School is due to start in a little over two weeks from now. I guess I better start getting my stuff ready! Everything is happening so fast. I am so excited!

God to me:

> I have created you for great things (Ephesians 2:10). You are not your failures. Thank you for toughing things out and trusting Me. You will be so happy you chose to trust Me.

Thank You Lord for investing in me like You have; for believing in me when I stopped believing in myself; for being my strength when I was weak and broken; for continuing to set visions of hope before me; for sustaining me and fanning into flame the fire You placed inside my heart for You and Your purposes over four years ago; for giving me determination in the face of fear; for giving me the will to succeed and persevere. I know that with You I can do anything (Psalm 18:28-36; Matthew 19:26). I know that what You are doing inside of me and who You are is greater than I can even fathom. I choose to put my trust in You (Psalm 147:5; Isaiah 40:28, 55:8-9; Job 26:14, 36:26).

(July 17, 2005)

Sermon notes from Faith Assembly of God:

You cannot be committed to God without being committed to the things of God (for me, Master's). The world's comforts will steal your chances to be close to God if you let them (for me, the temptation to take the massage job and be financially secure instead of pursue Master's right now). When we turn to God instead of the world we will have a closer intimacy with God.

God desires this closeness. He desires for us to trust Him with everything. God desires true commitment from us. When we are truly committed, this is when we will really start making a big difference for Christ.

Yes Lord! I want to make a big difference for You. Thank You for making it clear to me what I need to do to accomplish this.

(July 19, 2005)

Sermon notes from "The Living Room":

We need to constantly evaluate our lives. In the Christian life, it's not how you start, it's how you finish. We can't allow ourselves to get struck down by the cares of this life (I was letting this happen to me over the past 10 months). It's a war. The odds are against us. Don't give up! Don't give in! God wants to give us life to the fullest (John 10:10). Our heart's cry from the time we are young to the time we are old needs to be, "God, I want to live for You!" Anyone can serve Jesus on the mountain top, but can you serve Him in the valley?

Thank you Lord that I can now say, "Yes, I can serve you in the valley." To You be all the glory. You are so faithful!

God to me:

> I know you want to live for Me. Oh My child, My precious, precious child, you will thank Me. The times I've told you,"No," the things you've laid down and surrendered to Me, you will thank Me. I know it's not easy, but trust Me when I say that I will more than make up for everything you've counted as loss. Thank you for trusting Me and surrendering those things to Me. I've been doing some major reconstruction in your heart and soul over the past several months. I know it

hasn't been easy, but it was necessary. Thank you for trusting Me.

Oh Lord, thank You for allowing me to rest in Your presence tonight. I can't tell You how thankful I am to feel close to You again. I missed You so bad! Thank You for giving me a renewed sense of courage, strength, and willingness to follow You. Thank You for all the amazing people You've placed in my life here to help me. You are so faithful and trustworthy.

Questions:

1. What are some of the trials Christians will face as they are obedient to live for God? Refer to Matthew 5:11-12; John 15:18-21; Acts 14:22; 1 Thessalonians 3:2-4; 2 Timothy 3:10-12; 1 Peter 4:1-4.

2. Would you say you are fully committed to the things of God and His plan for your life? Or have you let the comforts of the world (financial security, material possessions, physical pleasure, prestige, praise, etc.) steal away your chances to have a close intimate relationship with God?

3. What do you think it means to serve Jesus in the "valley"?

Chapter 34

(July 28, 2005)

Angel of the Lord:

The Lord delights in you greatly. I know He tells you this, but He wanted me to tell you too. He tells us about what a beautiful woman you are becoming and how much joy you bring to His heart. God sent us (some of His angels) because you asked for more. We have been watching you. We are aware you have been wrestling, trying to hold onto your peace and joy in the Lord. Thus says the Lord,"You are free." Now, concerning your future: because you have chosen to put your trust in the Lord, you are going to witness and be a part of a mighty revival that is getting ready to take place. There has been much set before you. All you need to be concerned with is keeping yourself pure and plugged into God. So that's what we are going to work on. **God has given you the ability to help people see that in Him they have what it takes to be all He created them to be.** Satan tries to blind people from seeing this. He's tried to blind you of this, but praise God, you

> have overcome! You have been given the ability to be a great leader. Jesus calls you friend. The world is passing away. Satan's demise is near. Bind yourself to Christ and to your brothers and sisters in Christ. There is strength in numbers. Clothe yourself in the armor of God (Ephesians 6:10-17). If you want to experience more victory, you need to do this more often. Your "flesh" is not your friend, it is your enemy. It's keeping you in bondage. If your freedom is really as important to you as you say it is, then you are going to have to put up more of a fight. Your hope in Jesus is real.

(August 16, 2005)

Last night we had a class meeting. All we did was share with everyone where we felt like we were at with God and with ourselves. Theresa (the second year girl's discipleship director) was leading our conversation, and she made only one request: "Be *real.*" Everyone really opened up. It was so powerful! Some people (including myself) cried.

I've been going through a hard time lately. I've been having feelings of wanting to run away and hide. I know it's my flesh, or sinful nature, that wants to run away and hide, and I know it's because I've been taking some big steps toward God. In nature, this sort of response is called the "fight or flight response." In this case, my flesh hasn't been doing so great in battle, so now it's trying to get me to run. I am *so* glad I am all the wiser regarding Satan's schemes.

Last night, it became even more apparent to me that God is not going to allow me to get any real kind of satisfaction or peace by anything other than Him. He's told me this several times, and I've prayed for it so, I'm thankful. One thing I've paid too much attention to for so long is how I look. I can remember a few times where I just let go and didn't care, and those were some of the best times ever. I am learning that true beauty is on the inside, and external beauty isn't that big of a deal (1 Peter 3:3-4). I know I've also depended on the approval and praise of other people too much. I am learning how shallow these things are, and that I need to seek to please God alone and let His love for me be enough (Galatians 1:10; 1 Thessalonians 2:4).

Oh Lord, Thank You for not giving up on me. Thank You for being so patient with me. I have known the valley, not to the depth others have known it, but to me, it's been enough. Thank You for rescuing me, forgiving me, and strengthening me. I love You so much!

"God is faithful, who has called you into fellowship with his Son, Jesus Christ our Lord" (1 Corinthians 1:9). How many times have I said this? And it's so true! I am here getting closer to Jesus and pursuing full-time ministry. God has been faithful to keep me like He said He would. Glory be to God!

Questions:

1. Make a list of some things that could steal away someone's peace and joy in the Lord. How can these be avoided?

2. Describe what it would look like for someone to stay pure and plugged into God. Refer to Psalm 119:9.

3. What has Christ set us free from? Hint: read Galatians 5:1-6.

4. Write down Ephesians 6:10-17 in your own words.

5. Make a list of characteristics of your "flesh" or "sinful nature." Include a few Scripture references.

6. Write the definition of "sanctify." Now write down 1 Thessalonians 4:3-4.

7. What does it mean to be beautiful on the inside? Refer to 1 Peter 3:3-4.

8. What do you think it means to have a gentle and quiet spirit?

9. Why it's so important to seek to please God alone?

10. What need are people seeking to satisfy when they seek the approval and praise of other people? What is the only way this need can truly be satisfied?

11. Why is it so hard to stand on God's Word sometimes?

12. What do the "flaming arrows of the evil one" look like (Ephesians 6:16)?

Chapter 35

(December 24, 2005)

So I've been home for Christmas break for a week now, and I haven't been having a very "jolly" time. I say this, because it feels like from the moment I arrived in Ohio, I've been in constant fighting mode. This might sound extreme, but it sure feels true enough. I have been battling with several things since I've been home, but my biggest battle has been with discouragement. I occasionally struggle with this, but since I've been home, it's been pretty constant. I know a lot of my discouragement stems from the fact that not long after I arrived in Ohio, I found out that Mom and Dad are separated. Dad told me this when he picked me up from the airport. I knew my mom and dad had been struggling, but I didn't know it was this serious. My dad and I talked about it for almost the entire two hour ride home. He's really heart broken. He told me that he didn't see it coming. My mom hasn't mentioned divorce, just separation. It doesn't seem good, though, and Dad said that he's not going to wait around in limbo forever, not knowing what she's going to decide. I've realized that my dad is battling with a lot of the same things that I am, but to a greater degree. I want to help, but I know it's something they need to work through themselves. I am really struggling with all of this.

God, please help me get my emotions under control. Please help me trust You with my family and myself. I know You have all the answers, which is both comforting and frustrating at the same time. I've just been really discouraged lately. You know what is best God. Let Your will be done, in Jesus name, amen.

God to me:

> My daughter, You've been ruined for anything less than what I have for you. Don't worry. Just keep coming to Me for comfort and direction and trust that I will help you continue to grow. And trust Me when I say you are growing. Peace, My child. Trust Me with your parents. I love them just as much as I love you, and that's A LOT!

(January 6, 2006)

So I'm still struggling with discouragement, but thankfully not to the degree that I was during Christmas break. So, why am I still struggling? I guess I've been having a hard time trying to perform well at school and deal with my parents' separation at the same time. Not preforming well at school tends to wear on my confidence level—thus the cycle of discouragement continues. So how can I break free from this cycle? God's told me that I'm not my failures, and that I need to trust Him with my family. It's just *really* hard, especially because it seems like things are getting worse. This has all been a major test of faith. I know it's my choice. I can either choose to stand on God's promises and have peace, or doubt and be discouraged.

Please help me Lord. I need You.

On a happier note, I am excited to report that by me receiving God's grace and comfort to the degree that I have, I was actually able to help my dad with some things he's been struggling with! Obviously, what he is going through is way more difficult, but I have noticed some similar themes going on: discouragement and feeling like a failure. It makes me think about the portion of

Scripture in 2 Corinthians 1:3-4 that says, "Praise be to the God and Father of our Lord Jesus Christ, the Father of all compassion and the God of all comfort, who comforts us in all our troubles, so that we can comfort those in any trouble with the comfort we ourselves have received from God." God is *so* good! I feel better already!

Sermon notes from Faith Assembly of God:

Fear of failure is one of the most powerful weapons the devil can use to keep us from doing things for God. He will try really hard to get us to believe that we aren't good enough, or that we're gonna mess up. A lot of people give up before they even try. You will miss one hundred percent of the shots that you don't take. It's important to have a plan before you run, but when God says it's time… go for it!

Deliverance is a partnership with God. Sometimes God doesn't come to our rescue because He believes we have it in us to defeat whatever it is we are up against. We have to take up the armor of God and put it on (Ephesians 6:13-17). God has given us power and the authority to use that power (Luke 10:19). We will stand in victory if we stand on His Word (1 John 5:4).

Thank You Lord, for helping me to grow up spiritually, and for confirming through this sermon what You have been speaking to me about not being afraid to mess up, and about standing on Your Word.

(January 15, 2006)

Sermon notes from Faith Assembly of God:

The storms that usually take us down or wear on us are the ones that happen when we are lacking divine direction; and when we are living a Christ-less life. We need to understand our purpose, and we need to walk close with Christ. We try so hard to straighten out our lives on our own, but WE NEED CHRIST!

There is no way we can live a victorious life without Christ. We need to understand that God is always with us. Jesus is waiting for us to recognize His presence. God does not compromise His Kingdom. He will not honor disobedience. Busy people will be distracted and aggravated by people who understand, recognize, and live in the presence of God.

Oh Father, help me to understand, recognize, and live in Your presence more. I need You so bad. Thank you. In Jesus precious and mighty name, Amen.

Questions:

1. How do you deal with discouragement and depression?

2. Write down some advice you would give to someone who is struggling to take control of their emotions.

3. What is one of the most powerful weapons the devil can use to keep us from doing things for God?

4. Do you struggle with the fear of failing? Have you let it hold you back from moving forward? If so, stop it! Put your trust in the Lord, for He cares for you, and move forward!

5. Why does God sometimes not deliver us from our trials right away?

6. Write 2 Corinthians 1:3-4 in your own words.

7. Make a list of some things you tend to do to straighten out your life on your own.

8. What is your purpose/ life mission/ calling? If you are not sure, write what you think it is.[12]

Chapter 36

(January 22, 2006)

So, what I am about to say may come as a shock. It did to everyone here at Master's anyway. It even caught me off guard, because I thought I was doing better. It didn't catch God off guard, though. He knew what was really going on inside of me; He knew the intense spiritual battle I was still in with one of my biggest fears: failure. What I am referring to is how I quit Master's Commission for a few days. I had wrestled with the idea of quitting Master's earlier in the school year, and I thought it was out of my system, but it came up again this past week, even stronger. This whole experience was *really* difficult, but I am really thankful for it because God used it to address some areas of sin in my life and give me an increased measure of spiritual freedom.

So, as I have already mentioned in previous journal entries, I have been struggling with several things lately. The biggest ones have been my parents' separation and my own insecurity. God has been telling me over and over again that I need to look to Him for my strength and stand on His Word, trusting Him with all of these things. At times I would be successful, but it seemed like after a few days, or a few poor attempts, my focus would shift from Jesus back to my problems. This was a vicious cycle. It's no wonder I was struggling so much, and I gave up for a little bit. I felt like I was at a crossroad yet again. Was I going to trust God nd do things His way, or was I going to keep trying to do things in my own way, in my own strength?

Everything came to a head this past Sunday morning during Sunday School. Pastor Johnny, the youth pastor, was talking to the youth staff about how to be a good youth leader. As he was going down the list of how to be a good youth leader, I started to become increasingly discouraged because I didn't feel like I was fulfilling *any* of the requirements. On top of that, it was overwhelming for me to even think about trying. I had already been really discouraged that morning about not doing well with other things, and this experience just topped it off. I felt like a complete and utter failure.

My first response was to blame others. After all, most of the people that I would cry to about my inadequacies told me that I was doing fine, so of course it was their fault I was failing so badly, right? Of course not! Believing that I was doing fine was me taking the easy road out. This caused me to continue on in my unhealthy ways of trying to do things my own way, in my own strength. I knew that I needed to stop doubting God and giving into the desires of my flesh, and that I needed to be more consistent with standing on God's Word and putting Him first. But it was just so hard! I had never experienced such an intense battle between my flesh and my spirit. All I wanted to do was feel better, and for too long my flesh was getting the upper hand. God has made it clear to me that if I put other things before regularly meeting with Him and reading the Word, then I am doing things in my own strength. This has been one of my biggest struggles ever since I first committed my heart to the Lord. God knows how bad I want to succeed in this area, and how important it is for me to do so. I know this is why He has been allowing me to go through all of this.

As soon as class let out, I quickly made my exit. I quickly made my exit, because I knew if I stayed any longer I would burst into tears, and I didn't want anyone to see me cry. I didn't want anyone to see me cry because I didn't want anyone to tell me that I was doing fine. I let myself believe this lie for too long, and I didn't want to live in that lie any more. I knew I couldn't continue on in this way if I wanted to move forward in God's plans for me.

One of my classmates did actually end up noticing that I was upset, and followed me outside. I didn't say anything to her until we got outside. All I said when we got outside (through tears) was that I just wanted to take my Bible and go to a desert island by myself. After I said this, she told me what I didn't want to hear: that I was doing fine and to not be so hard on myself. When she finished telling me this, something inside of me snapped. My sadness turned into rage and I quickly got up and stormed to our classroom. My friend followed me and kept asking me what was wrong. All I said was, "I'M DONE!" I was now in full on defense mode.

I needed to feel close to Jesus again, and soon; I knew if I didn't, I would *really* lose it. In this moment, I had come to the conclusion that I couldn't feel close to Jesus and be in Master's at the same time. Of course this is what the devil wanted me to believe. One of the main purposes of Master's is to draw people closer to Jesus, and it *was* drawing me closer to Him. It was actually drawing me *very* close, I just couldn't see it because I was so consumed with how uncomfortable I was. One of my excuses for leaving Master's was that I felt like I was too busy doing stuff *for* Jesus to have a close relationship with Him. I knew that the relationship had to come first. I had tried and tried to balance the two and it just wasn't working for me. For a while I kept pressing on, hoping it would eventually get better. Obviously it got worse. I was running on low trying to do things in my own strength for a long time and God finally let me run out of gas.

At the time, I saw leaving Master's as the only solution to my problem of not feeling close to Jesus. I know now that Master's wasn't what was keeping me from being close to Jesus. My problem was that I was trying to do things in my own strength and putting other things, like the satisfaction of my fleshly desires (sleep, entertainment, and socializing) before spending adequate time with Jesus. I realize now that I had a sufficient amount of time in Master's to get close to Jesus, I was just being selfish and not using it wisely. I will explain how I came to this conclusion in a minute.

It was invigorating driving to my home opener's house that morning. It felt similar to what I imagined it would be like to break out of prison. It wasn't long after I returned to Joy's house that my cell phone started ringing and people came knocking on the door. I ignored them. I wasn't about to let anyone drag me back into the prison I felt like I had just escaped from. When I told Joy that I had decided to leave Master's Commission and explained to her my reasons why, she didn't try to sway me either way. She just listened and said she was there for me.

The next day, I went in to talk to Pastor Darryl to let him know I was okay and to explain my decision to leave. I told him that I left so that I could get closer to God. He didn't say much. How could he argue with that? He did say that he was there for me if I ever needed him, though, and that he was inspired by me. It felt weird to hear him say that last part. In hindsight, I am super inspired by *him*. How he handled this whole situation was so wise—a mark of true spiritual maturity.

The next day, Jesus let me know that He was pleased that I wanted to get closer to Him. He then showed me in a very creative, and might I add entertaining, way that finishing Orlando Master's Commission *was* in fact part of His plan for me; that as much as I didn't want to, I needed to go back.

God then showed me in a very gentle and kind way that what I was doing by leaving Master's was giving into my flesh and running away from hardship. He made it clear to me that if I wanted to move forward in His plans for me to be a leader, then I needed to stop doing this. I needed to learn to deny my flesh and embrace the hardship of what He was calling me to do and trust Him to be my joy and strength. I knew that accepting this was the only thing that was going to help me move forward and grow in my faith (James 1:2-8). I am reminded of my recent unhealthy dating relationship, and how God was speaking very similar things to me. I knew it was time for me to nip this bad habit in the bud. After I went back through my journals and saw all of the times that God had made it very clear to me that attending Orlando Master's Commission *was* His will for me, I knew I had truly been deceived. I had fallen into the devil's trap, and I know now that it was because I was really struggling. Instead of running to God for help, I reverted back to some old habits: being led by my emotions, protecting my pride, and trying to do things in my own strength (being selfish). I can't say God didn't warn me.

What God was asking me to do by following through with Masters was *really* difficult. At the time, I did *not* want to do it. But after I had my time with Jesus (which I know was vital), and I realized that I had been deceived by the devil, I felt a renewed sense of strength and drive to get back in the ring. I say this, because like I said earlier, it feels like I have been in an almost constant fighting mode.

I know now that the main reason God let this happen was to fully expose just how *not* good enough I really am and how desperately I need Him *every minute of every day,* completely tearing down any sense of pride in myself that I might have. Everything that is good in me is from Him (James 1:16-18). This just shows how much I've struggled with pride. I know I've obtained a greater measure of spiritual freedom in this area, which I'm *really* excited about, and I can say with all honesty it was totally worth it! Pride is such a lie! We are all in desperate need of God. If the devil can get us to believe we don't need God, then in many ways, he has won.

So, now to explain the entertaining part. Wednesday morning, I decided to watch the animated DreamWorks motion picture *Madagascar.* It wasn't long into the movie that I started to notice some similarities between what I was feeling and what Marty, the main character, was feeling. He wanted to get back to his roots, but he felt trapped. That's why I left Master's! I felt like being in the program had caused me to lose the ability I once had to be close to Jesus. I realize now that God was teaching me how to walk close with Him in the busyness of life, and how to depend on Him alone and not in my own strength. This is clearly a very important lesson that I needed to learn, and I can't learn something by removing myself from the very thing that has been placed in my life to teach it to me. In this case, it was Orlando Master's Commission.

So anyway, as I was watching the movie, I was feeling pretty good about my decision to leave Master's, up until the point where things started to go south for Marty. He had succeeded in breaking out of the zoo, and he thought he was alone until his friends showed up to rescue him. He told them that he didn't want to be rescued (sound familiar?). But it was too late because, unbeknownst to them, they had attracted a crowd of police and animal rescuers. The police and animal rescuers felt Marty and his friends were too dangerous to return to the zoo, so they put them on an ocean liner that was headed for a nature reserve. However, the ocean liner was hijacked by some very clever, freedom-hungry penguins from the zoo, and the crates that Marty and his friends were in fell off the boat into the open ocean. They all ended up washing ashore on the island of Madagascar.

This was ideal for Marty. His friends were not so happy about it though. In fact, at first they were really mad at him for taking them away from the safety and comfort of the zoo. He told them they didn't have to come after him, but they didn't see it as an option because Marty was their friend. It didn't take long for them to start to really enjoy the wild though. Well, all except for Alex, their leader. It took him a little bit longer to let his guard down and really embrace the wild. When he did, though, something happened to him that he and his friends didn't expect. Truly embracing the wild brought out the not-so-nice side of Alex, the side that made him want to *eat* his friends! Toward the end of the movie, they heard a boat coming and rejoiced because it meant they were saved. Alex refused to go with them though, because he didn't know when he might turn and try to eat his friends. He wasn't willing to risk this because he loved his friends *too* much (again, sound familiar?).

Now for the best part! As everyone, except for Alex, was running for their lives toward the boat, Marty turned around. He couldn't just leave his best friend to die! He *knew* that Alex had a good heart and wouldn't eat him. As Marty ran back to where Alex had barricaded himself behind stone bars, the dreaded foosa started to chase after him. The foosa were the most feared and deadly animals in the jungle. Marty cried out to Alex for help At first, Alex covered his ears and tried to ignore his friend's cries for help. He did this because he didn't see himself as any better than the foosa. Then, after hearing Marty cry out to him for help several times, it was like a light turned on in his brain, and he saw that he *wasn't* just like the foosa. Like the powerful, noble, righteous lion that he was, he came to his friend's rescue. Shortly after this, the rest of the gang showed up and *together* they defeated the foosa. Wow! I wonder if the person that wrote this movie knew how many powerful parallels to certain elements of Christianity it contains.

I saw Pastor Darryl (and myself to an extent) as Alex, and my other leaders as Marty's friends. They tried to steer me in the right direction, and I know they were fighting for me in prayer. The foosa were like demons lying in wait to attack me when I was alone (the devil tries to get us alone, as he knows we are more vulnerable when we are alone). I saw the wild as the world, and the zoo as God's Word, or His will for my life. God's Word is there to keep me safe and help me live a better life. I might feel like I am missing out on something better, but I am really not. Every temptation in the world only leads to hurt and heart ache nd unfulfilled desires in the end. I have learned this the hard way many times.

God to me:

(After I watched *Madagascar*)

> Master's is your cross. Full-time ministry is your cross. It will not be easy. Anything outside of this will."Choose this day whom you will serve (Joshua 24:15).

Later that day, I went back through my current journal and paid special attention to the times where God told me that it was His will for me to do Master's, warning me to not let doubt in. Oops! There was also one particular thing that I had written down recently that jumped out of the pages at me and gave me chills as I read it. It's the passage of Scripture in Luke 22:31-32 that says, "Simon, Simon, Satan has asked to sift all of you as wheat. But I have prayed for you, Simon, that your faith may not fail. And when you have turned back, strengthen your brothers." When I read this, I knew that I had just been sifted like wheat by Satan, but to the praise and glory of God my faith didn't completely fail. Jesus helped me to repent and turn to Him again. After God showed me this, I knew I needed to share everything I had just gone through and the lessons learned with my classmates, so that they could be strengthened and built up in the faith. I felt that it was my responsibility, and the least that I could do to thank God for everything He had just done for me.

I returned to class on Thursday. I found out when I returned that my classmates were really shaken and hurt by my leaving. I wasn't even thinking about how my actions might affect other people. I guess I didn't realize how much influence I had. I asked Pastor Darryl if I could speak to everyone on Friday morning so I could explain why I left, share what God had shown me, and apologize for hurting anyone. He said, "Yes." I basically shared everything I just wrote down, and afterward we watched Madagascar! It was invigorating to do what I knew God had told me to do, and be that open with everyone.

Lessons that I have learned, or that have been reinforced through this experience:

1. I can't live a life of faith in my own strength. I need Jesus. I need to stand on the Word.
2. Rules aren't so bad. They are there for my good.
3. God will take care of me and will guide me down the right path when I am sincerely seeking Him.
4. Don't let problems build up. Seek help, and not just from people that are going to tell me what I want to hear. Talk to people who are going to be honest with me and tell me the truth in love—people who are going to ask me the hard questions, give me biblical advice, and help keep me accountable. Also, don't feel bad about asking for help.
5. Take a break every so often even if I don't think I need one.
6. Filter all of my feelings and thoughts through God's Word, and get wise counsel.
7. I've got the courage inside to radically trust God (yay!!!).

Questions:

1. How did this chapter speak to you?

Chapter 37

(January 24, 2006)

God to me:

> It's not over yet. Breathe. I'm taking My sword to certain areas in your life that are impure. You need to go through this. You will feel weak for a while, but I will renew your strength. I am purifying you from false securities. I will teach you and fill in the voids. I will give you solid things to hold on to. Keep giving Me your all.

"He will sit as a refiner and purifier of silver; he will purify the Levites and refine them like gold and silver. Then the LORD will have men who will bring offerings in righteousness," (Malachi 3:3).

"Therefore, since Christ suffered in his body, arm yourselves also with the same attitude, because whoever suffers in the body is done with sin. As a result, they do not live the rest of their earthly lives for evil human desires, but rather for the will of God" (1 Peter 4:1-2).

Angel of the Lord:

> You will be the least vulnerable to attack when you remember and stand firm in who you are in Christ. Remember: you are holy and anointed; you are called; you are set apart; you are forgiven; you hold authority in the heavens; you are a child of God; you are a warrior; you are a leader; you have been employed by God to restore and build His Kingdom; you have been commissioned to fight; you are strong. People are walking around lost and dead inside. YOU CAN HELP! Don't believe the lie that you can't. All you have to do is submit to God and allow Him to work through you. He will give you the words to say and show you what you are supposed to do. He will cover you if you mess up. Nothing is a mystery to God, and as you surrender more and more to God, your path won't be a mystery to you either. Always remain surrendered to Him and willing to learn.

(January 29, 2006)

Sermon notes from Faith Assembly of God:

All of us will experience bitter pools in life (Exodus 15:22-27). Sometimes God will lead us to bitter pools. Why would God lead us to bitter pools? To purify us of things we need to get out of our lives. Life is too short to live by a bitter pool. We need to get up and praise God! Praise makes God bigger in our minds and it shows faith. He *is* a BIG God. God wants us to trust Him. Bitter pools expose our true character. God will test us until we deal with our bitter pools and trust Him. This is for our good. Moses cried out and the Lord showed him what to do. This is our key. When we cry out to God, He will show us what to do. He is no

.especter of persons (Ephesians 1:18; James 1:5). God will supply for our needs (Matthew 6:25-33).

We need to throw Scripture into our bitter pools, we need to sow some good seeds. Life is filled with bitter pools. Problems will come to us all. Just HOLD ON! God will use adversity to make you the person He created you to be. If a chisel isn't good enough, He will use a sledge hammer. If a sledge hammer isn't good enough, He will use a bulldozer. What is going on inside of you is a whole lot more important than what is going on outside of you. Focus on God in your pain and you will go through your pain. Focus on your pain and you will stay in it.

When we worship God when we are hurting and don't understand, our praise is never more pure. Romans 8:28 doesn't say everything works together how you want it. It says, "Everything works together for the good of those who love him, who are called according to his purpose." If you don't love God, then everything is working together for your bad. We need God. God is not going to give up on us. He is going to keep trying to get our attention and help us. You only fail if you don't get back up.

Oh Lord, thank you for strengthening me and confirming again through this sermon all the things you have been speaking to me about the trials I have been facing lately. I am so in awe of You. You are so wonderful, amazing, and good!

(February 16, 2006)

So, last night around 12:30 a.m. I checked my email, and I got an email from my dad that said to call him. The date on it said February 16, which concerned me because he doesn't normally stay up that late. I know he's been really struggling with what's going on with him and Mom. We've talked a lot about it. They've been separated for over a month now, and I know it's tearing him apart. I feel really bad, but at the same time, I can see how it's been so good for him. I can also see how it's positively affected those under him, specifically me and my siblings. Mom is still undecided about what to do. She told my dad that she's going to move out in the beginning of March (my dad is currently living with my Uncle Dan). It doesn't seem real. God's hand has been evident over everything, though. I've seen God make Himself known to my dad in a deeper way, and it's so beautiful to see. It seems like he is truly finding God.

I've really enjoyed my conversations with my dad lately. They've been very rich and meaningful. One time, we even talked on the phone for two hours, which is a lot for my dad and I. Before this our phone conversations were normally only between five and ten minutes long, if that. Another incredible development is that Dad and Michael are actually getting along, and even enjoying each other's company again! They haven't had a good relationship since my brother was 15, maybe even younger. Also, my dad's been reading Christian books and praying a lot more too. He even went to a charismatic Catholic healing service. He said that when they anointed him with oil and prayed over him, his knees started knocking and his hands started shaking. Then he said he went and knelt down for a little while, and "the tears were flowing." He is currently going with my uncle Dan to a "40 Days of Purpose" meeting once a week at a nondenominational church in Sandusky called "The Chapel." He said that he's really been getting a lot out of it. He told me that some of the things they've said have really hit him, like the fact that God knew they were all going to be there before they went. Then he said, "So does that mean He knew your mom was going to leave me?" It's really got him thinking. God is so faithful, because I can see how He's making my dad into the man of God that I know in his heart he wants to be. This is an amazing answer to prayer.

Questions:

1. Write down the definition of "purity".

2. Do you feel like God wants to purify you of anything right now? If yes, what is it? If no, just in case, pray and ask God if there is anything.

3. Who are we in Christ? Hint: John 1:12, 15:15; Romans 6:18; 1 Corinthians 3:16, 6:19, 12:27; 2 Corinthians 2:15, 5:17, 20-21; Galatians 2:20; Ephesians 2:10; Philippians 3:20; 1 Thessalonians 5:5; 1 Peter 2:9-10; 2 Peter 1:4. Write down at least three of these scripture references.

4. Read Exodus 15:22-27. What did you learn about God from this Scripture?

5. What is your first response when you are struggling? Is it grumbling like the Israelites when they came to the bitter pool, as is the case with most people when they face difficulties and trials? Try crying out to God like Moses did, and also pray and ask God if there is anything He wants you to change. Either way, continue to praise God. Praise will carry you through the difficulties and help you to remember that God is in control (Romans 8:28).

Chapter 38

(April 5, 2006)

I finished my last journal by saying that I wasn't accepted as a third year student at Orlando Master's Commission, so I will start this journal by recounting Pastor Darryl's reasons for not accepting me. They were really quite profound, as well as very healing and liberating. (I wasn't exactly sure if I was supposed to do a third year or not, so I figured I would just apply and take the results as the answer.)

Pastor Darryl told me that he thinks I've moved past a lot of what they are doing here, and he feels like if he were to bring me back, it would paralyze me. I feel that way as well, but I've gone back and forth about it, trying to decide whether or not I was just being prideful.

Next, Pastor Darryl said, "This is how I see it. You are accustomed to swimming in the ocean. That's where you feel most free, and being in Master's, for you, is like being at a dry dock. I think you came here to get some patchwork done, but once that patchwork has been done, it's back to the ocean for you." He went on to say that he feels like God brought me here to build up my self-esteem and strength, and to regain trust in Him and His people (other believers). Then he told me that he felt like I had come a long way, and that by graduation, he feels like I will be ready to set sail again. My hands immediately flew up in the air in excitement! I felt so energized. Everything Pastor Darryl said was everything I wanted to hear. Finally, he gave me his blessing and told me that he appreciated me, he knew how much I appreciated him and the program, and that he would miss me. In my mind, things couldn't have gone better.

I feel very accomplished and ready to face the world again. This year was *extremely* hard, but it was all *so* worth it. I will be forever grateful for everyone here who so warmly welcomed and received me. They have all enriched my life so much. I told them they were all like precious jewels that God has given me to put in the treasure box of my heart.

After Pastor Darryl and I finished talking, I went away by myself and talked with God while Pastor Darryl finished meeting with everyone else. During this time, God told me to read Proverbs 3 frequently. After I read through it, I realized He gave it to me to help me stay on course, kind of like a compass. So cool!

Lord, thank You so much for all You've done in me this year; for wounds healed, faith strengthened, vision clarified and expanded, friends made, and roots deepened.

(May 18, 2006)

So, it's three days until graduation! Everything feels so crazy. We have so much to get done, which makes it hard to be excited. It's probably just one final test. I honestly don't know what I'm going to do the day after graduation, except take my dad and younger sister Janet to the airport. I am really glad they're coming!

I've been up and down a lot lately. I know God has worked in me a lot this year, and I want the work to be completed. So, if I need to experience a few more down times and hardship so the work can be completed, then so be it. I know that in hindsight I will appreciate this year so much more than I do right now, and right now, I already appreciate it a lot!

Even though this year was really hard, I also *really* loved it. I can say with all honesty that it has been both the worst and the best year of my life so far. I have publicly announced that the biggest thing I felt like I got out of this year was the faith that I needed to truly believe that *I am who God says I am*. The truth that *I am not my failures* has been so deeply ingrained in me over this past year; for this, I am deeply grateful.

Questions:

1. Read Proverbs chapter 3. Now choose three of your favorite verses from this chapter, write them down, and memorize them.

2. Write the definition of "trust."

3. Make a list of things that distract you from accomplishing your goals.

4. Would you say that, for the most part, you are a confident person? If yes, why? If no, why not?

Chapter 39

(June 28, 2006)

So much has happened over the past month. It's been one month and one week since I graduated from Orlando Master's Commission. Graduation was really nice. It was hard to really enjoy it at times, because we crammed so much into the last week, including a lot of last minute preparations for graduation (it was a big production), bonding time, and heartfelt farewells. We were all *so* exhausted. We didn't necessarily feel prepared for the actual ceremony part of graduation, but everyone who was there said that it was really good—which was a huge relief for everyone involved. After it was all said and done, I was really thankful for the experience. I felt very accomplished.

It was really nice having Dad and Janet here. They stayed for about four days. I was really hoping they would have a good time, especially Dad, because he's been so depressed about what's happening with him and Mom. By this point, Mom had moved out and told him that she wanted to get a divorce. I was a little nervous to see him, because I didn't know what to say. Everything turned out great though! I know that Joy played a big part in that. She and Dad had a lot of long, heartfelt conversations, which involved plenty of encouragement and honesty. I think some of the honesty parts were hard for my dad to hear, but I know he was really appreciative. He said that, at this point, he just wants things to get better, no matter what that looks like. I just hope he continues to keep this attitude.

Last I heard, it's hard for him to be in the same room as my mom, and he does everything he can to avoid this from happening. He's definitely been getting a major dose of humility lately. I think our whole family has been getting a major dose of how fickle and weak we all are as humans. I can see how God has been using all of this to help us not only become healthier as a family, but also more humble as individuals. I just hope that my mom and dad get some healing, work out their differences, and get back together eventually. Either way, I know I need to keep trusting God.

After Dad and Janet left, I kind of secluded myself from everything for about a week. I didn't go to any church functions, except the church service the Sunday after graduation with Joy and her mom. I only talked to a few friends to let them know I wasn't going to be at cell group that Tuesday. I was *so* exhausted. I slept a lot, and just sat and thought about my life and how I've gotten to where I am, and where God might be leading me next. I didn't really get very far, though. I just don't know what to do. I feel like I'm being pulled in two very different directions. I'll explain in more detail momentarily.

As I mentioned earlier, my biggest struggles this year were a lack of confidence in myself and in God in certain areas. I felt like I was almost constantly fighting thoughts that were telling me that I wasn't good enough and that I would just fail. I realize now that *I* will never be good enough, but the amazing part is—I don't have to be. Jesus is the only one who ever was or will be perfect and I am made righteous and perfect by His sacrifice on the cross for me—and for all who call upon His name (2 Corinthians 5:21; Romans 10:13). God has made these truths very evident to me many times, especially this year. He's also made it very evident to me that with Him all things are possible, and that He *is* in fact with me and will not ever leave me or forsake me (Mark 10:27; Deuteronomy 31:8; Hebrews 13:5). I just need to keep believing this. I also need to keep believing that I am who He says I am. I am starting to understand the power of faith at a deeper level, and learning just how crucial faith is to our success as Christ followers. The beautiful part about faith is that, if we are lacking it, all we need to do is ask God, and He will give it to us (James 1:5-7)!

Speaking of faith. One day, during morning devotions towards the end of the year, I had a vision of myself in a cage, and I noticed that I had the key to get out. Even crazier was the fact that I saw that the door was open, but I wasn't walking through it! This really disturbed me. I knew that Christ died to set me free, and I've heard Him tell me over and over again that I really am free, hence the open cage. My heart's cry, ever since I first became aware of this fact, has been to walk in this freedom and help others do the same. I know that the only way I can help others walk in freedom, though, is by walking in it myself. There have been times that I have walked in this freedom, but it's only been for moments at a time. This shouldn't be—I don't *want* it to be anymore! I know that the only way I can consistently walk in freedom from the power of sin is by following the guiding of the Holy Spirit; standing in faith on God's Word, that through Jesus' death and resurrection I am free from the power of sin and death (Ephesians 6:13-17). I have learned that truly believing this makes all the difference in the world—the difference of being caged or free.

Moving right along. I went to Ohio to visit my family in the beginning of June, and not surprisingly, it was *really* difficult. Here is a copy of a letter I wrote to a "special friend", whom I will introduce you to in a moment. *The plot thickens…*

(June 7, 2006)

Dear "special friend,"

Well, I'm still feeling a little weird about things here at home. I haven't seen my mom yet. I was supposed to see her last night, but I decided against it. I know this upset her, but I just wasn't ready. I was able to talk to her calmly over the phone before I got home, but when my dad drove me past her apartment to show me where it was, and I returned home to see most of her stuff gone, it hit me pretty hard. I know I would have been a mess if I had gone to see her last night. I will see her eventually, though.

I've been fighting feelings of being really upset with her for leaving. I know that what's happening isn't all her fault, I guess I'm just really sad about the whole situation. It's really hard to hear my dad talk about it. He's really hurting. My mom hasn't talked about it much. I know she must be really hurting too. My dad feels like a huge failure. On top of this, he has a lot of stressful things going on with work, and he's about to turn 50! He said that he definitely thought things would be different for him at 50. I asked him where he imagined he would be. He said he was hoping to be out of debt and at least still have his wife.

I know that he feels horrible for all the hurt that he's caused, and he's apologized to my mom, but that obviously isn't enough this time. She needs to see a real change on his part, which I think is completely understandable. I hate that things have gotten to this point, and I really want to help, but I know the best thing I can do is simply keep praying and giving it to God.

This is by far the biggest test of my faith I've experienced thus far—not struggling in my faith in Jesus of course, but struggling to hold on to all His promises. I know that I have a choice. I can either choose to let Satan steal my peace and joy, or I can trust God, rejoice through it, and believe that everything is going to work out for the best. It's just really hard, and my feelings are definitely fighting against trusting God. I just want things to go back to normal (if they ever really were normal), and I want the hurting to stop. But most of all, I want things to get better, whatever it takes.

Last night, after I had a good cry and asked God to help me, I felt very peaceful. Then, before I went to bed, I asked God what Psalm I should read. I heard, "Psalm 50." When I read it, verses 14 and 15 really stuck out to me: "Sacrifice thank offerings to God, fulfill your vows to the Most High, and call on Me in the day of trouble; I will deliver you, and you will honor Me." What I got out of these verses is what God has already spoken to me so many times: that I need to praise Him, even when it's really difficult, and continue to stand on His Word, trusting that He will work everything out for good.

So, now to introduce you to my "special friend," who is actually my boyfriend now. Yes, that's right, I said, "Boyfriend." "Do tell," you say? Okay, I will.

So, in the beginning of March, a team from Orlando Master's went to England on a mission trip, which included myself, of course. Tim (my now boyfriend) was one of the guys from the church we were working with in England that came to pick us up from the airport. This just happened to be the same church in Southport that Stephen (the guy I met on the flight to Orlando) is from! Tim is actually from South Carolina. He's been in England since the beginning of the previous summer, and has been working on staff at Shoreline Church since September. Part of his role has been to help with the oversight of the discipleship aspects of the Master's Commission program there.

When I first saw him, I got butterflies in my stomach. I immediately chastened myself, though, saying, "Focus, you're on a mission trip. No boys!" I found out later that God didn't want me to completely shut Tim out—it was just me being overly guarded. Don't get me wrong. I believe that it's very wise to be guarded, especially when it comes to romantic relationships. It's just not wise to let your fears hold you back. If God is giving you His approval, and encouraging you to move forward with something (or someone), then that's what you should do, fear and all, trusting that God will help you.

I did pretty good at first with keeping my guard up, but as time went on, I became increasingly lax about it. It didn't help that I could tell that he had similar feelings for me too! He didn't say as much, and he was careful to not make it too obvious. But as the days passed, it became increasingly obvious that he "fancied" me as well. Toward the middle of the trip, we often found ourselves chatting during breaks and sitting beside each other on the bus as we traveled from place to place. Now that I think about it, I don't think it would have been possible for us to ignore each other. It was like there was this invisible magnetic force pulling us together, and it felt very "right." I didn't recognize it then, but I know now that it was God drawing us together. Against my will (but not really), we exchanged contact details on a train ride before my team and I left England.

I'm not sure what I expected (or even wanted) to happen between Tim and I after I returned to Orlando. I mean, I did like him, but I wasn't trying to get into any serious dating relationships anytime in the near future. Not because I wouldn't have loved to find my prince and start our life together, but mainly because my parents were in the midst of divorce. I thought it would be extremely insensitive to start dating anyone in the near future, at least until things sort of cooled off between them. On top of this, Tim didn't really fit my description of the perfect mate for me. Notice I said "my." Something about letting go of the idea of Tim and I being together didn't feel quite right, though. I didn't really know what to do with this feeling, because I didn't expect it. Like I said, part of me didn't want it at the time, so I just pushed it to the back of my mind and tried to focus on school and getting closer to Jesus.

A few days after I returned to Orlando, I got a really random and silly online message from Tim, and those butterflies in my stomach started up again. I was surprised at how excited I was to hear from him. I promptly messaged him back, not thinking about the potential of a serious relationship forming between us. I think that my initial thought was that a friendly, fun, long distance relationship was a nice distraction from all the hardships I was facing at the time. Little did I know that it was God's intention for Tim to be more than a nice distraction for me.

Tim and I continued to message each other back and forth on a regular basis for a couple of months. In the process of getting to know each other, which was really fun, I was surprised at how similar our hearts for God and ministry were. I couldn't help but wonder, was he "the One"? I tried not to think about it too much, though. For one, we hadn't known each other for very long. Also, like I said earlier, my parents were in the middle of a divorce, and it felt extremely insensitive to even think about getting married anytime soon. I felt like it would be pouring salt on their open wounds. Then, at the end of April, during a morning prayer time, I had a very strong feeling that Tim and I's relationship would move in the direction of marriage, and soon. This feeling came after I asked God where He wanted Tim and I's relationship to go, and I very clearly heard Him say, "Just trust Me." Deep down, I knew this meant that He wanted us to be together, and sooner rather than later.

I felt very fearful and torn. Now, don't get me wrong, the idea of Tim and I being together was exciting to think about. But when I thought about how the reality of Tim and I entering into a serious relationship (that would soon lead to marriage) would effect my family, it was just too much for me to bear. I also know that another reason I was struggling with this was because I knew that if Tim and I got married, I would most likely end up settling in England. This pretty much cancelled out the likelihood of me and my best friend being neighbors like we talked about since we were kids. If this was God's plan, it was definitely not in my comfort zone, and didn't fit into "my" plans.

Then, one day, not long after God told me to trust Him about Tim, I explained to Him how being with Tim would mean causing my parents more heartache, and that as much as I really liked him, I just couldn't handle being the cause of more heartache for them. Then, without waiting to hear what God thought about what I just said, I acted on my emotions and fears and texted

Tim to let him know that I wasn't ready for a relationship. He messaged me back and said, "OK," and stopped messaging me.

I thought I would feel better, but I didn't. I did my best to try to forget about him though. I was doing pretty good too up until one morning during morning prayer, about a week and a half after I ended things with him. An overwhelming feeling of missing him came over me. I prayed about it, and heard God tell me not to be afraid to move forward in my relationship with Tim. I apologized to God for giving into my fears, and surrendered my heart and life to Him fresh and new, whatever that meant. It felt really good knowing that I was putting God first again.

After I fully surrendered my heart to God again, my affections for Tim grew almost instantly. It quickly became very clear to me, to my delight, that Tim was in fact the man of my dreams. I was confused at the timing of it all, and I felt guilty for being so happy while the rest of my family was so sad. At the same time, I was really excited. I texted Tim that day and told him that I missed him and to forget the previous message I sent him. He said that it was forgotten, but not really, because he felt we could learn from it. He then told me that he missed me too. He also said that no decisions needed to be made at that point regarding whether or not we needed to always remain friends or become something more. He said decisions like that could be made in due time, but that he didn't think it would be wise to make that particular decision just yet. He went on to say that he was definitely interested in getting to know me more, and it was his desire that our friendship would grow. This answer was fine with me. It was actually better. It took away any unnecessary pressure, and it actually made me like him more! (I hadn't told him what God had told me about us yet.)

The more I got to know him over the next couple of months, the more my affections for him grew, and the more excited I was about the potential of us being partners in life and ministry. After I graduated from Master's, Tim and I started to talk more openly about liking each other. I didn't say much to my family about our relationship and what was going on in my heart, due to all the reasons I've already listed.

Tim has been here in the States with me for a little over a week now. He flew over here to visit me on June 19. He is due to fly back to England in a few days. Our time together has been quite enjoyable. Expectations have been met and surpassed! We spent one week in Orlando, then we drove up to his hometown so I could meet his parents. I love it here! And I love his parents. It was here, today, on June 28, that Tim and I became an official couple. Oh, happy day!

Questions:

1. Why is it important for us to humble ourselves before the Lord? Refer to Proverbs 11:2, 16:18; Matthew 23:12; Luke 14:11; James 4:10.

2. What do you think it means that Jesus is the source of life? Include Scripture references.

3. Do you feel like your fears are controlling you? If so, name them, and ask God to help you overcome them. Write down your conversation.

4. Why is it important to not let our fears hold us back?

Chapter 40

(August 12, 2006)

I'm getting married!!! Tim proposed to me last night over the phone, and of course I said YES! He didn't plan on proposing to me over the phone, but that's just how it happened. It felt very freeing to finally talk about it and make a set decision regarding it.

Our conversation started off by him telling me that I would be receiving a very special package from him in the mail, and that I needed to make sure to read it all, especially the very end. Well, of course I was very curious, and I kept pressing him about what was in the package and what was so important for me to read at the end. He said that it was a surprise and he didn't want to spoil it. I told him that telling me wouldn't spoil it (I had a pretty good idea it was a proposal for marriage).

He eventually gave in and told me that he sent me a journal that he had been keeping since we first met, containing all the things he wanted to say to me about how strongly he felt about me; things that he didn't want to tell me right away because he thought it wouldn't be wise and it might scare me off. He told me that at the end of the journal was a proposal for marriage. The word "DESTINY" quickly flashed in my mind. Then, after a moment of sweet silence, with great joy and excitement I said, "Of course! I would *love* to be your wife." It felt so natural to say those words to him. I recognized it as the same feeling that

I felt every time I made a big decision to move farther into my destiny in God.

Tim will be here in exactly two weeks from today. The first item on our agenda is to go *ring shopping!* There have been times that old fears and doubts have tried to rise up, but my heart and mind are made up. I know these are heavy words, but it has been becoming consistently clearer for months now that this is the path that God has for me. This is my lot, and I love it! I enjoy it. I know it. I *choose* it. Like I said, I'm still a little nervous, but there's a boldness that has risen up inside of me that's greater than the nervousness I feel, and I know it's a direct result of the confidence that I have that God is leading me in this direction. "Lead us Lord" has been our constant cry, and lead us He has. I trust Tim. He makes me feel safe. He encourages me. He inspires me. He challenges me. He intrigues me. I am really looking forward to our life together. I feel confident that he will keep his promise to love and cherish me and always give God first place in our life together.

(September 16, 2006)

I feel like I'm in a season of letting go. What am I letting go of? I believe God is asking me to let go of *myself* at a deeper level. 2 Corinthians 5:14-15 says, "Whatever we do, it is certainly not for our own profit, but because Christ's love controls us now. Since we believe that Christ died for all of us, we should also believe that we died to the old life we used to live. He died for all so that all who live—having received eternal life from Him—might live no longer for themselves, to please themselves, but to spend their lives pleasing Christ who died and rose again for them." Yesterday I mentioned to Tim that I feel like I need to rededicate my life to the Lord. He asked my why, and I said that I feel like Jesus wants my relationship with Him to move to the next level, and that I feel that rededicating my life would help me move in this direction.

(October 9, 2006)

Yesterday morning at church, I felt the sweet, loving, comforting presence of Jesus wash over me for almost the entire service. I haven't felt the tangible presence of Jesus like this for a while, and it was so wonderful (and much needed). During this time, the Lord was reminding me of the work that needs to be done in the Church and the world, and of the role He has for me to play in it. He was also reminding me of how much He loves me, and how much He believes in me.

At the end of the service, during the prayer time, I felt impressed to go to a lady a few pews back from the front and ask her if she could pray for me. When she asked me what I would like prayer for, I told her that I've been struggling and feeling far away from the Lord, and that I feel like I need to rededicate my life to Him. It was weird to hear myself say this, because I know that I'm still a Christian. I've just felt so far away from Him lately. The only reason that I can think of that I've felt so far away is that I've experienced so much change lately, and I haven't gotten back into a good rhythm of spending time with Jesus. I know that I need to stay strong in my relationship with Him if I want to stand strong in the faith and feel close to Him. She prayed for me and led me in a prayer of rededication. It was nice, and just what I needed.

During Master's last year, I felt like God told me to forget familiar places. I feel like by making these recent decisions—to marry Tim, move to South Carolina, and help get a youth ministry started after we get married, that I've done this. I feel like, in a spiritual sense, by making these decisions I have jumped off a giant cliff—the cliff of familiarity and comfort into the "wild unknown", that place of complete trust. It was the boldness that it took, the ways that it would inspire others, and most of all the joy that it would bring to the heart of God that inspired me to jump. I didn't think of the mountains of pain and brokenness that I might have to face, or the deep valleys of doubt and despair, or the rivers of restlessness and failure, or the forest of past mistakes and temptations. That's probably a good thing, though.

This isn't the first time I've had to deal with these things. I can see very clearly now how God has been equipping and preparing me for this place, faithfully equipping me with tools and weapons and diligently teaching me how to use. I recall God telling me that the seeds of faith I planted in obedience would sustain me in the times to come. I am so thankful that I listened and was obedient to plant those seeds.

This is the place where faith is tested. I know that I'm not alone here. I know I will not die here. Even as I pen these words I feel God's grace keeping me, and His strength filling me, restoring in me the will to fight. I've said it before, and I am sure I will say it many times again: as painful as it is sometimes to surrender to God, it is *so* worth it! Even though I have been struggling lately, I have a deep sense of peace. I know yesterday's encounter with Jesus and the prayer session really helped with this.

(January 19, 2007)

This morning after I woke up, while I was still lying in bed, I replayed in my mind when I first met Tim. Afterward I thanked God for bringing us together. After I finished thanking God for bringing Tim and I together, I clearly saw in my mind's eye a large, unfinished puzzle. I knew that it represented the unfinished puzzle of my life. There were quite a few pieces that were fit in place, but there were also quite a few pieces that were still waiting to be put in place. Then I saw one of the puzzle pieces that was waiting to be put in place being placed into the finished portion of the puzzle. I knew it represented Tim.

After this piece settled in place, the blessed assurance that I'm on the right path, and that Tim and I are meant for each other, swept over me again like the gentle, relaxing breeze of a sunny spring afternoon. Directly following, a few lines from the chorus of a song by Charlie Hall started playing in my mind:

> Broken hearts would be healed, empty souls would be filled… alive to Jesus and dead to this world.[13]

I then heard God very clearly say to me:

> This is what's going to happen because you have decided to trust Me with your future, specifically in saying "yes" to choosing to join your life with Tim's through holy matrimony. Broken hearts will be healed, empty souls will be filled… alive to Me and dead to this world. You have allowed me to speak into your life and direct you down the path I've chosen for you."Your will, not mine" has been your cry. I've heard your cries, and you're on your way, My daughter. I have great plans for you and Tim. I have chosen you to be his helpmate. Love him always.

I know I just need to keep trusting God and keep trying my best to keep Him first, receiving His grace and forgiveness when I need it. It's when I start taking my focus off of God and eternity, and start focusing on the things of this world that I get into trouble. I must say, the pull from the world has been very strong lately. Mostly, the pull to take the easy road. In my case, not blatantly rebelling against God, but settling for living a lukewarm Christian life instead of living a radical, sold out life for Jesus.

I have learned that for the weaker, Satan swings big. But for the strong, he chisels away little by little at their faith, in not so obvious ways, slowly breaking down their defenses. One way is by making them too busy to spend time with God, or planting small seeds of fear in their weak points, thus making them more vulnerable to attack. This has happened to me more times than I would like to admit, but God has made me aware of it and has equipped me with tools, training me how to use them to defend myself against Satan's schemes. Master's Commission has helped me a lot in this regard. Knowing one's weaknesses (fears, for example) is a major weapon. Equally important is reading and meditating on the Word of God—especially Jesus' finished work on the Cross, praising and worshiping God (especially when you are struggling and it's the last thing you want to do), guarding what you see and hear, walking in righteousness and purity, and staying accountable to other believers. This is not an exhaustive list, but it's a good start.

(March 21, 2007)

So, I am getting married in *3 days!!!* And what a wonderful man of God that God has brought to me. I am so excited to join my life with his.

I've been told that getting married is the second most important decision that a person can make—the first being to put your faith in/surrender your heart to Jesus Christ. There are a lot of things that are uncertain about our future, but I have peace because, even though I don't know what our future holds, I know who holds our future. And He is good, and His love endures forever (1 Chronicles 16:34; Psalm 100:5; Psalm 136).

Dear God, I can't thank You enough for Your enduring, everlasting, awesome love for me, and for everyone for that matter! Thank You for your faithfulness in my life, and for helping me to become more and more aware of and rooted in Your great love for me and who I am in Christ. You are worthy of all my life and love, and I am proud to be Your child. Please help me to continue to become more and more like You so that I can more effectively mirror Your love to the world. In the precious and holy name of Your son, Jesus Christ, Amen.

Questions:

1. Who are we suppose to live to please? Refer to 2 Corinthians 5:14-15.

2. Why is it important to have a regular, strong devotion life (relational time with Jesus)?

3. Do you feel like God is asking you to trust Him more? If yes, with what? What would this look like in your life?

4. What are some of the positive results of choosing to trust God and stand on His Word?

5. Why is it important to know our weaknesses?

6. What is the most important decision that a person can make?

Conclusion

Do you know now? Do you *know* that God *loves* you and that He will *never* stop loving you, no matter what? He loves you with an awesome, fierce, undying love, and He will never stop trying to get you to believe and understand and rest in His great love for you. These are the main points that I want you to take away from this book. What I desperately *don't* want you to take away from this book is that your good works somehow give you more value in God's eyes and make Him love you more. This lie can so easily sneak it's way into our belief system. Yes, good works are important, but they shouldn't be your main focus. Your main focus should be having a close, personal relationship with Jesus Christ. Remember, you don't need to try to earn God's love. It's already fully and completely yours through Christ!

One of the conclusions that I've come to so far in my journey with Jesus is this: what pleases God the most is when we completely trust in Him and His unfailing love for us. I believe, and the Bible says, that when we do this, everything else will fall into place (Matthew 6:33). As a parent, I know just how true this principle is. I know the times my children don't listen to me are the times that they think that I don't have their best interests in mind. Children have a hard time understanding that sometimes what they want isn't always the best for them; and dare I say so do adults when it comes to obeying God. If we could just get to the place where we completely trust in God's unconditional love for us, then I believe that we won't have such a hard time obeying His commands—commands which He has put into place for our good, because He loves us! God knows this, and I believe this is why He places the message of His love on so many people's hearts. We *need* to get it people! We need to *really* believe that God passionately and completely loves us, for our good and for His glory! I am still working on this, and I have learned that I have to daily remind myself of it.

God is not going to love you any less if you disobey Him. If anything, when you disobey Him, He will pour out His love and affection on you even more: at least this has been my experience. It has also been my experience that the devil will try to make you feel like a worthless piece of junk when you mess up, but this just isn't true. You are valuable and precious to God, and He will *never* stop trying to help you understand and really believe this.

When I mess up, God doesn't give me a guilt trip, but instead He reminds me of how much I am loved by Him. At times, if I'm stubborn, there may be some discipline involved. I'm afraid that some people don't realize that God's discipline is an act of love; probably because oftentimes people discipline others out of anger, and not out of love (Proverbs 3:12; Hebrews 12:6; Revelation 3:19). I have learned that loving, godly discipline is a balanced combination of compassion and firm authority.

God has a wonderful, exciting purpose and plan for you, but I hope you are starting to understand that this shouldn't be your main focus. Jesus is the only one that can help you fulfill your purpose. *You need Him!* In the beginning of my walk with the Lord, He asked me to do whatever I needed to do to give Him first place in my life. Sometimes, this meant that I needed to stop what I was doing or delay my plans so that I could take the time get some healing and rekindle a close relationship with Him. I believe that God has made room for this in His plans for us. In fact, this is a major part of His plan for us. It is vital that we take the time to understand who we are in Christ and learn how to rest in that.

What does God's love for me look like? What does it feel like? How do I know I have really taken God at His word, believing that He indeed loves me? I hope that as you read through my story and saw how these questions were answered for me, you were able to see clearly the answer to these questions for yourself.

Much love, Jennie

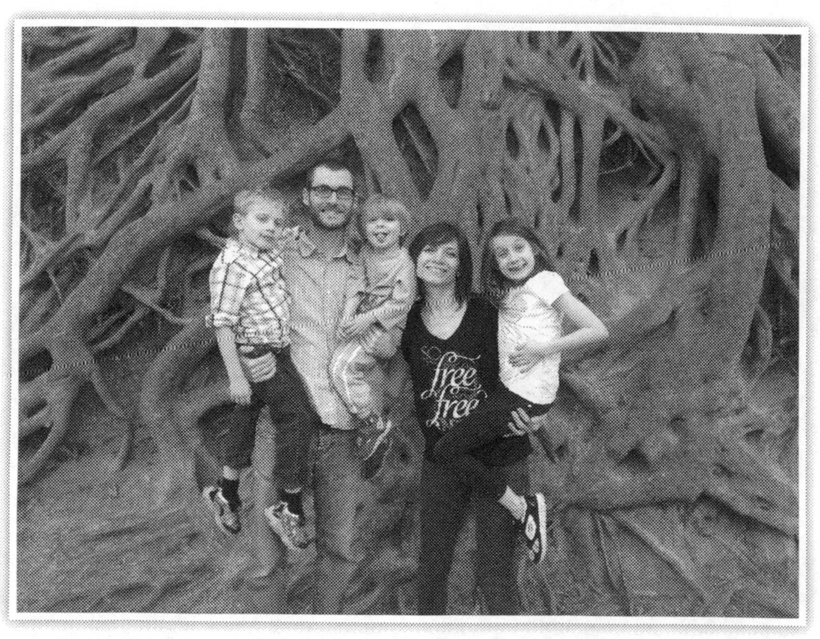

My 'Love', my babies, and me.

Endnotes

1 "Who is the Holy Spirit?", Got Questions Ministries, http://www.gotquestions.org/who-Holy-Spirit.html#ixzz3WFW4xR9L, October 9, 2015.

2 John Piper, "This Is He Who Baptizes with the Holy Spirit," Desiring God, October 9, 2015, http://www.desiringgod.org/sermons/this-is-he-who-baptizes-with-the-holy-spirit.

3 Sandie Freed, "Open the Floodgates and Expect an Open Heaven," Identity Network Inc., http://www.identitynetwork.net/Articles-?blogid=2093&view=post&articleid=25771&fldKeywords=Open%20the%20Floodgates&fldAuthor=Sandie%20Freed&fldTopic=0, October 9, 2015.

4 James J. Gettel, "Reaching Out to Others Transforms Us," MiddleVoice.com, October 9, 2015, http://middlevoice.com/PDF/Reaching%20Out%20to%20Others%20Transforms%20Us.PDF.

5 Visit www.mypersonality.info/spiritual-gifts/ to help you with this question.

6 John Piper, "The New Testament Gift of Prophecy," Desiring God, http://www.desiringgod.org/articles/the-new-testament-gift-of-prophecy, October 9, 2015.

7 Margaret Feinburg, *God Whispers*, March, 2002, United States of America, Relevant Books, p. 58.

8 Recommended read: *The Prophetic Ministry* by Rick Joyner.

9 Recommended source: Focus on the Family's "The Truth Project."

10 John Newton, "Amazing Grace," published 1779.

11 Recommended read: *Boundaries in Dating* by Dr. Henry Cloud & Dr. John Townsend.

12 Recommended read: *Chazown* by Craig Groeschel.

13 Charlie Hall, "Don't Pass Us By," Porch & Altar, Sparrow Records, 2001.

Printed in the United States
By Bookmasters